Readings in Radical Psychiatry

Readings in Radical Psychiatry

by
CLAUDE STEINER
HOGIE WYCKOFF
JOY MARCUS
PETER LARIVIERE
DANIEL GOLDSTINE
ROBERT SCHWEBEL
and
MEMBERS OF THE
RADICAL PSYCHIATRY CENTER

GROVE PRESS, INC., NEW YORK

ISBN: 0-394-17868-8
Grove Press ISBN: 0-8021-0042-2
Library of Congress Catalog Card Number: 73-21038
Designed by Stevan A. Baron
First Evergreen Edition, 1975
Manufactured in the United States of America
Distributed by Random House, Inc.
GROVE PRESS, INC., 53 East 11th Street, New York, New York 10003

Contents

Section I
Manifesto

Manifesto

by Claude Steiner

1. The practice of psychiatry has been usurped by the medical establishment. Political control of its public aspects has been seized by medicine and the language of soul healing (ψυχη + ιατρεια) has been infiltrated with irrelevant medical concepts and terms.

Psychiatry must return to its non-medical origins since most psychiatric conditions are in no way the province of medicine. All persons competent in soul healing should be known as psychiatrists. Psychiatrists should repudiate the use of medically derived words such as "patient," "illness," "diagnosis," "treatment." Medical psychiatrists' unique contribution to psychiatry is as experts on neurology, and, with much needed additional work, on drugs.

2. Extended individual psychotherapy is an elitist, outmoded, as well as non-productive, form of psychiatric help. It concentrates the talents of a few on

a few. It silently colludes with the notion that people's difficulties have their sources within them while implying that everything is well with the world. It promotes oppression by shrouding its consequences with shame and secrecy. It further mystifies by attempting to pass as an ideal human relationship when it is, in fact, artificial in the extreme.

People's troubles have their source not within them but in their alienated relationships, in their exploitation, in polluted environments, in war, and in the profit motive. Psychiatry must be practiced in groups. One-to-one contacts, of great value in crises, should become the exception rather than the rule. The high ideal of I–Thou loving relations should be pursued in the context of groups rather than in the stilted consulting room situation. Psychiatrists not proficient in group work are deficient in their training and should upgrade it. Psychiatrists should encourage bilateral, open discussion and discourage secrecy and shame in relation to deviant behavior and thoughts.

3. By remaining "neutral" in an oppressive situation psychiatry, especially in the public sector, has become an enforcer of establishment values and laws. Adjustment to prevailing conditions is the avowed goal of most psychiatric treatment. Persons who deviate from the world's madness are given fraudulent diagnostic tests which generate diagnostic labels which lead to "treatment" which is, in fact, a series

of graded repressive procedures such as "drug management," hospitalization, shock therapy, perhaps lobotomy. All these forms of "treatment" are perversions of legitimate medical methods which have been put at the service of the establishment by the medical profession. Treatment is forced on persons who would, if let alone, not seek it.

Psychologial tests and the diagnostic labels they generate, especially schizophrenia, must be disavowed as meaningless mystifications, the real function of which is to distance psychiatrists from people and to insult people into conformity. Medicine must cease making available drugs, hospitals, and other legitimate medical procedures for the purpose of overt or subtle law enforcement and must examine how drug companies are dictating treatment procedures through their advertising. Psychiatry must cease playing a part in the oppression of women by refusing to promote adjustment to their oppression. All psychiatric help should be by contract; that is, people should choose when, what, and with whom they want to change. Psychiatrists should become advocates of the people, should refuse to participate in the pacification of the oppressed, and should encourage people's struggles for liberation.

PSYCHIATRIC DISTURBANCE IS EQUIVALENT WITH ALIENATION WHICH IS THE RESULT OF MYSTIFIED OPPRESSION.

PARANOIA IS A STATE OF HEIGHTENED AWARENESS. MOST PEOPLE ARE PERSECUTED BEYOND THEIR WILDEST DELUSIONS. THOSE WHO ARE AT EASE ARE INSENSITIVE.

PSYCHIATRIC MYSTIFICATION IS A POWERFUL INFLUENCE IN THE MAINTENANCE OF PEOPLE'S OPPRESSION.

PERSONAL LIBERATION IS ONLY POSSIBLE ALONG WITH RADICAL SOCIAL REFORMS.

PSYCHIATRY MUST STOP ITS MYSTIFICATION OF THE PEOPLE AND GET DOWN TO WORK!

—Claude Steiner

(*Note:* The first Radical Psychiatry Manifesto was written in the summer of 1969 on the occasion of the annual American Psychiatric Association Conference in San Francisco, which was widely disrupted by members of the Women's Liberation, Gay Liberation, and Radical Therapy movements.)

Section II
Theory

1. PRINCIPLES by Claude Steiner[1]

Psychiatry is the art of soul healing. Anyone who practices the art is a psychiatrist. The practice of psychiatry, usurped by the medical profession, is in a sad state of disarray. Medicine has done nothing to improve it; as practiced today, medical psychiatry is a step sideways, into pseudo-scientism, from the state of the art in the Middle Ages when it was the province of elders and priests as well as physicians.

Psychiatry as it is predominantly practiced today needs to be changed radically, that is, "at the root."

Psychiatry is a political activity. Persons who avail themselves of psychiatric aid are invariably in the midst of power-structured relationships with one or more other human beings. The psychiatrist has an influence in the power arrangements of these relationships. Psychiatrists pride themselves on being "neutral" in their professional dealings. However, when one person dominates or oppresses another, a neutral participant, especially when he is seen as an authority, becomes an

---

[1] All of the articles in this book are reprints with minor changes of articles which first appeared in *The Radical Therapist* in 1970–1971.

enforcer of the domination and his lack of activity becomes essentially political and oppressive.[2]

The classic and prime example of this fact is found in psychiatry's usual role in relation to women where, at worst, psychiatrists promote oppressive sex roles and at best remain neutral, therefore supportive of them. The same is true of psychiatry's traditional role in relation to the young, black, and poor; in every case psychiatry's "neutrality" represents tacit support of the oppressive status quo.

There are four types of psychiatrists:

Alpha psychiatrists are conservative or liberal in their political consciousness and in their practice and methods of psychiatry; the largest majority of medical psychiatrists fall into this category.

Beta psychiatrists are conservative or liberal in their politics and radical in their methods. Examples of this type are men like Fritz Perls and Eric Berne and the human potentialities psychiatrists, usually not physicians, who expand the boundaries of psychiatric practice, but tend to be unaware of the manner in which oppression is a factor in psychic suffering and thus ignore the political nature of their work.

Gamma psychiatrists are radical in their politics but conservative in their practice. Examples of this are Laing and others (as a special case, Szasz whose awareness of the politics of psychiatry is quite heightened) who practice old, out-moded methods of therapy based on Freudian or neo-Freudian theory with emphasis on individual psychotherapy, "depth," and "insight."

The fourth kind of psychiatrist is the radical psychiatrist, who is radical both politically and in his psychiatric methods.

The first principle of radical psychiatry is that in the

---

[2] For an argument demonstrating the political nature of neutrality, liberalism, or tolerance read "Repressive Tolerance" by H. Marcuse, in *A Critique of Pure Tolerance* (Boston: Beacon Press, 1969).

absence of oppression, human beings will, due to their basic nature or soul, which is preservative of themselves and their species, live in harmony with nature and each other. Oppression is the coercion of human beings by force or threats of force, and is the source of all human alienation.

The condition of the human soul which makes soul healing necessary is alienation.[3] Alienation is a feeling within a person that he is not part of the human species, that she[4] is dead or that everyone is dead, that he does not deserve to live, or that someone wishes her to die. It may be helpful, in this connection, to remember that psychiatrists were originally known as alienists, a fact that seems to validate the notion that our forefathers knew more about psychiatry than we. *Alienation is the essence of all psychiatric conditions. This is the second principle of radical psychiatry.* Every psychiatric diagnosis except for those that are *clearly* organic in origin is a form of alienation.

The third principle of radical psychiatry is that all alienation is the result of oppression about which the oppressed has been mystified or deceived.

By deception is meant the mystification of the oppressed into believing that she is not oppressed or that there are good reasons for her oppression. The result is that the person, instead of sensing his oppression and being angered by it, decides that his ill feelings are his own fault, and his own responsibility. The result of the acceptance of deception is that the person will feel alienated.

The difference between alienation and anger about one's oppression is unawareness of deception. Psychi-

[3] The view that man's alienation is the result of mystified oppression stems from Marx.

[4] In order to avoid the sexist connotations implicit in the use of solely masculine pronouns such as "he" and "his," we have throughout this book deliberately included "she" and "her" as well.

atry has a great deal to do with the deception of human beings about their oppression.

Oppression + Deception = Alienation[5]

Oppression + Awareness = Anger

EXAMPLES

Consider a seventeen-year-old American youngster during the Vietnam war. He is told that he must offer his life to destroy the enemy in Asia. He is told that this is good for him, for his brothers and sisters, for his country, and even for the enemy. He is taught that a man will defend his country without question, and that a man who hesitates or questions this principle is a coward who does not deserve to be called a human being. If he fails to understand that he is being oppressed and if he believes these lies, he will eventually come to think of himself as less than human for not wanting to defend his country. He will doubt his own opinions and experiences concerning the war. He will come to consider himself a coward; he will become disgusted with himself; he will cut himself off from his peers and will become depressed. He may lose interest in everyday activities; he may begin to speak about hopelessness and meaninglessness; he may start using drugs to give himself a temporary reprieve from his despair. If his shame and despair reach large enough proportions, he may attempt to destroy himself. He will see himself as no good and will believe himself in need of psychiatric attention.

If he were to consult a "neutral" therapist, he might be asked, "What is wrong with you? Why are you de-

[5] Thanks are due to Hogie Wyckoff for her contribution to the development of Radical Psychiatry's basic formula.

pressed? Why do you hate your father? Why do you rebel against authority? Let's talk about it, and you'll feel better. Tell me about your childhood. Maybe the bad things that happened then make you sad now. Other boys your age aren't depressed about the war and killing. These are troubled times, but others are able to adjust to them. Why don't you? Tell me your dreams. Maybe we can find what is wrong with you. The army is bad, I know, but it has its good points. It might make a man out of you."

This young man may eventually feel better because of the friendly and warm attitude of the therapist, thus mystifying his true feelings about the war. He may "pull himself together," his personality-trait disturbance (passive-aggressive, aggressive type) may improve, and he may wind up in a flag-wrapped box. His therapist will feel and will contend that he was neutral throughout the therapeutic intervention and that he did not attempt to influence the young man. But in truth he acted as a recruiting officer for the army, all the more effective for his disarming smile.

It is awareness of the oppressive quality of "neutral" psychiatric intervention that keeps most of the oppressed young, black, and poor away from psychiatrists who, they know, will behave as if no oppression were occurring. Neutrality in an oppressive situation is equivalent to oppression; scientific detachment in a concentration camp is support for the murderers who run it.

A radical psychiatrist will take sides. He will advocate the side of those whom he is helping. The radical psychiatrist will not look for the wrongness within the person seeking psychiatric attention; rather, he will look for the way in which this person is being oppressed and how the person is going along with the oppression. The only problem that radical psychiatry looks for inside someone's head is how he empowers and enforces the lies of the oppressor and thereby enforces his own oppression.

The classic and prime example of the oppressive role of psychiatry is found in its usual relation to women, where at worst psychiatrists promote oppressive sex roles and at best remain neutral, therefore supportive of them.

Take, for example, a woman who lives with a man who dominates her in every way, including treating her as a sexual object. The assumption of their sexual relationship is that she will have intercourse with him any time *he* wants it, while he has no particular responsibilities or concern for her pleasure. If she achieves orgasm, fine; if she does not, they agree that orgasm is not a necessary ingredient of female sexual pleasure. If this woman becomes "frigid" and talks to a radical psychiatrist, she will say to her, "You have as much right to sexual pleasure as he. If you do not achieve orgasm, it isn't because you are frigid but because he is selfish. Don't make love unless you want to, and demand to achieve orgasm at least as often as he does. There is nothing wrong with you except that you're accepting his domination and that you are justifying it; so that instead of seeing that you're quite right in not enjoying sex, you have come to the conclusion that you are 'frigid.' "

METHODS

What, then, are the methods of radical psychiatry? *The radical psychiatrist sees anyone who presents himself with a psychiatric problem as being alienated; that is, as being oppressed and deceived about his oppression, for otherwise he would not seek psychiatric succor.* All other theoretical considerations are secondary to this one.

The basic formula of radical psychiatry is:

Awareness + Contact = Action → Liberation

The formula implies that for liberation two factors are necessary: On the one hand, *awareness*. That is, awareness of oppression and the sources of it. This type of awareness is amply illustrated by the writings of Laing and the writings by radical feminists and blacks, and gays. However, this formula also implies that pure awareness of oppression does not lead to liberation. Awareness of oppression leads to anger and a wish to do something about one's oppression; so that a person who becomes so aware changes from one who is alienated to one who is angry in the manner in which some black people and women have become angry. Anger, therefore, is a healthy first step in the process of liberation rather than an "irrational," "neurotic," or otherwise undesirable reaction. But liberation requires *contact* as well as awareness. That is to say, contact with other human beings who, united, will move against the oppression. This is why it is not possible to practice radical psychiatry in an individual psychotherapy context. An individual cannot move against his oppression as an individual; he can only do so with the support of a group of other human beings.

Still, awareness and contact cannot yield liberation except through some form of *action*. Only action by groups of people who have become aware of how they are oppressed will lead to *liberation*.[6]

Thus it appears *radical psychiatry is best practiced in groups* because contact is necessary. Because people seeking psychiatric help are alienated and therefore in need of awareness, *a radical psychiatry group seems to require a leader or leaders* who will undertake to guide the liberation process. To avoid the leader's oppression of group members *each individual member should propose a contract with the group* that indicates his wish to

---

[6] The element of *action* was added to the formula by collective decision of the members of the Radical Psychiatry Center.

work on a specific problem. Liberation from the leader's guidance is the ultimate goal of radical psychiatry and is indicated by the person's exit from the group.

Contact occurs between people in a number of different forms. Basically, contact is human touch, or strokes, as defined by Berne. But contact includes also when people become aware of their oppression, as well as permission, and protection.

Permission is just what the word implies, a safe-conduct for a person to move against his oppressor and to "take care of business." This permission needs to come from a person or persons who at the moment feel stronger than the one who is oppressed, usually the leader. Along with the permission, the person who is to move against the oppression also needs to know that he will be protected against the likely retaliation of the oppressor.

This, then, is the vital combination of elements in radical psychiatry: awareness to *act* against deception, and contact to *act* against alienation. It should be reemphasized that *neither awareness by itself nor contact by itself will produce liberation*. As an example, it is very clear that contact without awareness is the essence of the therapeutic encounters of the "human potentialities" movement. The potency of human contact and its immediate production of well-being, such as found at Esalen and within the "human potentialities movement," is rightfully eyed with suspicion by therapists in the Movement because, without awareness, human contact has a capacity to pacify and reinforce the mystification of the oppressed. It is equally clear that pure awareness, whether it be psychoanalytic or political, does not aid the individual in overcoming oppression, since the overcoming of oppression requires the banding together of the oppressed.

2. ALIENATION by Claude Steiner and Hogie Wyckoff

Alienation is a term that is commonly found in psychiatric writings, especially in relation to youth, the poor, and minorities. The word "alienation" in this context is referred to in the sense of "being apart from the main group, out of the mainstream, a state of estrangement; of being far removed or inconsistent with. . . ."

We believe that this is the shallow meaning of the word. For a more meaningful interpretation of alienation one must refer to Marx and his *1844 Manuscripts;* an interpretation which has as its indispensable elements oppression and mystification.

ALIENATED LABOR AND NEEDS

Marx believed that as people produce objects in their labor they are producing themselves; that is, people come to know themselves as producers of objects. This is also the way in which people master their world. They find their meaning in their labors, and when their labor becomes fragmented and meaningless or when the means of production and decision lie in the hands of others (e.g. capitalists), labor becomes alienated, and the person loses his sense of mastery and meaning; that is, the person becomes alienated.

In the Marxian sense, alienation is not just being separate from others as it is being separated from oneself, one's human potentialities, one's labor, one's intelligence, one's capacity to love, or one's body—and it is always seen as the result of the mystified acceptance of oppression.

One of the most meaningful human needs is the need to be creative and effective in mastering one's environment. Yet, today, people are alienated from the satisfaction of this need and instead are isolated and stunted by doing labor for wages which is largely meaningless to them and over which they have no real control. People sell their time and energy at a job which requires them to expend themselves and to forgo effective control over the total process of production. People are required to be passive in crucial ways while they are allowed to be active in meaningless ways. People work on parts of a whole, never getting closure, and are intentionally kept as cogs in the corporate wheel, made to feel ineffectual—and ultimately powerless. Workers find little satisfaction or joy in their labor and are told such meaning must be sought in leisure, a passive nonwork where they attempt to gain satisfaction as consumers of things and services, rather than as doers.

When people are alienated from meaningful labor, fragmented, cut off from each other and forced to be competitive, they also become alienated from other people. Having been cut off from the meaning in communal social relations, they are forced by the bleak alternatives made available to them into developing a false need to try to escape, to buy the means of forgetting the pain and emptiness of their working lives, to dream of being human through fantasies created by the media's seduction, and to struggle for attainment of objects that are imitations which approximate and create a caricature of real humanness and human happiness.

People's needs, above and beyond the most basic needs for food, shelter, and clothing, are not permitted to spring forth naturally from them, but are manipulated by external powers over which they have no control, like the media, advertising, and fashion.

As an example, a worker on an automobile assembly line who works eight hours a day and spends two hours commuting to her place of work has a real need for transportation. Communal public transportation is made unavailable, so that this real need for transportation which was created by her work becomes her own individual responsibility. She can only fulfill this need through the expensive personal purchase of one of the automobiles she has had a meaningless and alienated, and yet essential, part in producing. She now finds herself in a place where she creates a part of a part of an object and is later seduced (if not actually forced) into purchasing it. This car which she has helped build and which is totally alien from her will, turns on her in the form of exorbitant monthly payments, repairs, taxes, etc., so that it becomes necessary to deal with it on its own terms, to be passive in relation to it rather than active as would be the case if she had built the whole machine and could fix it herself, in which case she could have some pride of craftswomanship for her labor as well.

When our labor is not alienated, the power of the object becomes an extension of our power. The object we create does not turn against us or deplete us, but rather adds to us. Thus, our labor becomes a positive force rather than a potential enemy.

In order to combat alienation it is necessary that we get back in touch with our underlying or truly felt needs and that we break the strangle hold of advertising and fashion upon our appetites. Human needs cannot just be accounted for in terms of material things, although this is a value the capitalist system desires to instill in us, since making money is its only motive. We are manipulated and corrupted in our desires because they are created by others for their benefit rather than for our own. We must break the bonds of the consumer culture on us and expose the false promise of individul liberation through the acquisition of commodities for the empty lie that it is.

Our real, felt needs can only be clearly identified once we begin to fulfill them because we are so detached from them now. Through a growth process beginning with partial solutions, a gradual rediscovery of them can develop. We must remember the social character of human needs—needs for cooperation, contact, support, love that cannot be bought and sold.

Marx saw thought as alienated when it is merely abstract, speculative theory, not grounded in action or practice: that is to say, when it is separated from being actually tried out in the world.

People can separate thoughts from action and not test them in reality. But any thought which keeps us from action is alienated. The psychiatrically disturbed or behaviorally incapable who are not able to be effective in the world are extreme examples of the alienation of thought. But we are *all* being taught in different, subtle ways to be behaviorally incapable.

In the midst of the severe alienation from our human potentiality, we are being tricked into believing that we have real choices because as consumers we can supposedly choose between the kinds of goods that we purchase or the politicians that we elect to office. These choices are, of course, not providing us with real freedom, but are rather diversions that keep us pacified and prevent us from actively seeking actual liberation.

ALIENATION AND RADICAL PSYCHIATRY

In radical psychiatry we see all psychic difficulties as forms of alienation. People at this historical moment are to one degree or another alienated from their real needs and potential. Most people are oppressed (coerced through force or threats of force) away from autonomy and wholeness as human beings, and are mystified about their oppression. This oppression is based on keeping people incomplete and not fully satisfied so that they will be willing and highly motivated consumers and exploitable workers. We believe it is necessary for psychiatry to make people aware of this oppression; to demystify it and to create sensibilities against it in people so that they will recognize it and refuse to continue to suffer it.

In the same period in which Marx was speaking about alienation in relation to labor, the word "alienation" was used in relation to the "mentally ill or deranged," and those who were their caretakers were called "alienists." The word "alienist" eventually became the word "psychiatrist," as the medical profession put its imprint on it as one of the medical specialties.

The sense that we (based on Marx) ascribe to alienation is intimately connected with mystification: that is to say, a sense that something is wrong and that there is no understanding of what is wrong; that the process that has caused the alienation has become opaque and not understandable to the person. This sense of alienation is especially apt in the case of so-called paranoid schizophrenia. The paranoid's experience is that there is something wrong in the world, something that he does not necessarily know or understand; that she is in some way persecuted and that she feels alienated from reason, from herself, and from others. His alienation includes ineffectual alienated thoughts, e.g. delusions which are impotent attempts to break through the mystifications that surround his oppression, in an effort to make that which is opaque more understandable. One of the tenets of radical psychiatry is that paranoia is the result of heightened awareness, an attempt by the mystified oppressed to explicate or make clear the mystified oppression under which they labor. The paranoid's experience of being persecuted is oppressed and the oppression of her experience is mystified.

The sense that we (again based on Marx) ascribe to alienation is also intimately connected with oppression, as in the case of the assembly-line worker who is pressed into unsatisfying labor, the product of which is taken away from him, and deceived into believing that rather than being oppressed he is truly fortunate in being able to use his earnings by purchasing a late model automobile, the colors, accessories, and horsepower rating of which he has *complete* freedom to choose. When this worker's automobile breaks down in the midst of heavy traffic on his way to work, he will not see himself as a victim of oppressions designed to satisfy the greed of certain privileged persons in society, but he will in all probability be mystified into seeing himself as the cause of his quandary. He will blame himself for not knowing how to repair his car, or for not having taken his car to a mechanic before it broke down, or for not having been able to afford a more expensive model, and so on. He will feel isolated from the thousands of others in similar circumstances and see them as competitors and enemies. He will feel depressed or angry, and he will vent his mood on his family, thereby transmitting the oppression downward in the hierarchy and away from its source.

The oppression of human beings begins early in their lives. The capacities of loving, thinking, enjoyment, and production are systematically attacked by parents and schools. Children, the most oppressed within each class of human beings, are enjoined against the expression of the need to "make" things, against the free exchange of strokes, against the full enjoyment of their bodies, and most significantly because of the need to mystify these injunctions, against the use of their capacity to understand and experience the world as it is. Parental and societal injunctions are eventually incorporated by the person in the form of the "Pig Parent" which, like a chronic implant in the brain, controls people's behavior according to an oppressive scheme. The acceptance of these injunctions is the only thing that is wrong with persons seeking psychiatric aid. The rest of the difficulties must be found in the person's external world.

OUR BODY

We are separated and oppressed away from our bodies, especially from our capacity to enjoy bodily pleasure. As Marcuse points out, Freud's oral/anal/genital scheme of erotic development is really an imposition upon a much more natural development which leaves the body capable of enjoying erogenous pleasure. According to Marcuse, we are forced to concentrate our pleasures in the genitals in order to free the rest of our body so that it may be readily oppressed in labor. Separated from our bodily sensations we are capable of suffering the abuse of alienated labor. We cease to feel either pleasure or pain. Our musculature becomes cramped as it is increasingly devoted to defensiveness rather than action or pleasure. We are told from childhood that things that are pleasurable are bad for us and that something that is unpleasurable is likely to be good for us, and we come not to expect pleasure from our work. By the time we have grown up we cannot enjoy the rhythm of our functions, the movement of our muscles, the sensations in our skin—we are, in short, alienated from our bodies. Separated from our bodies we engage in alienated sex and drug abuse in an effort to regain some semblance of bodily pleasure and experiences.

Drug abuses, from cigarettes to heroin, are attempts to re-establish contact with our bodies; the man who is sitting at a bar reminds one of a person who puts a dollar in the slot of a machine in an amusement park and receives in exchange for that dollar fifteen minutes of communion with his body. A shot of whiskey makes the cold, stony body feel, briefly, like a newborn baby's. Cigarettes do the same thing on a lesser level, and heroin is the ultimate drug for re-establishing touch. Heroin is, as most addicts will attest, unsurpassed in its capacity to produce feelings of well-being for its users. Unfortunately, drug use for the purpose of regaining touch with the alienated body becomes complicated by the fact that most drugs of this sort, except perhaps marijuana, are addictive, so that a larger and larger dose must be taken which has an increasingly lower effect; so that, in time, they become ineffective in breaking down alienation as they become increasingly lethal to the body.

Based on this point of view, radical psychiatry's approach to the abuse of drugs is focused on breaking down body alienation. This process is basically one of permission to *feel.* One of the great factors in drug abuse, naturally, is the promotion by the media of tobacco, alcohol, and other drugs. The main incentive for the oppression of people away from their bodily pleasure is to create a labor force which will submit to alienated work conditions, but drug companies constitute the supporting cast in this situation, providing as they do pacifying doses of de-alienation, for a price. Eventually, the drug companies have become as powerful an influence in the maintenance of bodily alienation as are those who wish to exploit human labor. In any case, these forces conspire heavily against any person's chance of growing up in our culture without being alienated from her or his own body.

OUR MIND

Alienation from our mind is a state of affairs commonly called schizophrenia. The schizophrenic was the alienist's principal customer. Ronald Laing, in his writings, covers this form of alienation quite thoroughly. In brief, he observes that it seems necessary for groups of people, especially families, to prevent individuals within them from expressing or being in touch with their own experiences of the world; and that this process is one which invalidates or makes invalids out of people so that those who insist on maintaining their point of view are tagged as schizophrenic or deviant and driven mad in a systematic conspiracy. Laing sees psychiatrists as acting in a naive collusion with the powers that be in policing individuals who show any sign of not relinquishing their experiences of the world in favor of the official version of it.

An extreme example of this type of alienation is paranoid schizophrenia. Varying degrees of being crazy, feeling crazy, or acting crazy are lesser manifestations of mind-alienation. The radical psychiatrist's approach to this difficulty is to align herself squarely with whatever the person experiences, and to teach people how to recognize and deal with discounts which are the transactional operation whereby people are invalidated. In the most extreme situation of paranoid schizophrenia the approach is to accept as a given truth that the person who is paranoid is being persecuted in approximately the way in which she claims to be, and to investigate the exact dimensions of the persecution. Validation of a person's experience of being persecuted, combined with protection from the persecution, results in a reinstatement of the valid connection between people's experiences and thoughts and what *in fact* is going on around them.

OUR LOVE

Human beings are not only separated from their bodies and their capacities to think, but also from their capacity to love others. Human love and warmth are essential for the survival of human beings. Berne has restated that fact in terms of the concept of strokes. Steiner's paper, "The Stroke Economy" (Chapter 3), describes in detail the manner in which human loving is alienated away from human beings. Briefly, our capacity to love is enjoined against and regulated and then turned against us in order to exploit us. People who are stroke-starved will do anything: work, buy, tolerate pain, in order to obtain strokes.

Increasing levels of stroke starvation leads from the commonplace "cruising" of the lonely young and the agitation which is observable in most people to the withdrawal commonly called clinical depression and, finally, to catatonic withdrawal in which strokes are not accepted even when offered. This continuum of stroke deprivation is related to by radical psychiatrists through making strokes available to the deprived by creating free stroke economies in groups and by teaching people in them to ask for, give, accept, and reject strokes freely.

The above three forms of alienation, plus alienated labor, are not seen by radical psychiatrists to be all-inclusive. They are arbitrary categories chosen at this point in time as being the most understandable and reasonable; and while they cover the gamut of psychiatric "psychopathology," they are obviously not complete and are capable of being improved.[1] In any case, the notion is that all psychiatric disturbance represents some form of alienation which in every case is the result of the oppression of a human capacity which is then mystified.

---

[1] For an exhaustive description of these three forms of alienation and their therapy, see *Scripts People Live*, by Claude Steiner (New York: Grove Press, 1974).

3. THE STROKE ECONOMY

by Claude Steiner

In *Games People Play,*[1] Eric Berne says: "Liberation is only possible at all because the individual starts off in an autonomous state: that is, capable of awareness, spontaneity, and intimacy." Colloquially, this statement reads: "Children are born princes and princesses and their parents turn them into frogs."

The theses of this chapter are:

1. That the method used by parents to turn children into frogs derives its potency from the control of strokes, so that a situation in which strokes could be available in a limitless supply is transformed into a situation in which the supply is low and the price parents can extract for them is high.

2. That the re-claiming of awareness, spontaneity, and intimacy requires a rejection of the parental teachings or "basic training" regarding the exchange of strokes.

3. That people's submission to their early basic training in relation to the exchange of strokes produces a population of stroke-hungry persons who spend most of their waking hours procuring strokes; they are therefore

[1] Eric Berne, *Games People Play* (New York: Grove Press, 1964).

easily manipulated by persons who control the supply of strokes through a monopoly of them.

In *Games People Play,* speaking about stimulus hunger, Berne says: "A biological chain may be postulated leading from emotional and sensory deprivation through apathy to degenerative changes and death. In this sense stimulus hunger has the same relationship to survival of the human organism as food hunger." The notion that strokes are, throughout a person's life, as indispensable as food is a notion that has not been sufficiently emphasized. Therefore, I wish to restate the fact: *strokes are as necessary to human life as are other primary biological needs such as the need for food, water, and shelter—needs which, if not satisfied, will lead to death.*

As Berne pointed out in the chapter on strokes in *Transactional Analysis in Psychotherapy,*[2] control of stimulation is far more effective in manipulating human behavior than brutality or punishment. Thus, while a few families still use brutality in an attempt to control their offspring, most injunctions are enforced in young persons through the manipulation of strokes rather than through physical punishment.

Previous writers have linked the control of vital human processes with broader economical and political points of view. Two such will be reviewed here: Wilhelm Reich and Herbert Marcuse.

Reich, as Berne, saw man at his deepest level to be of "*natural* sociality and sexuality, *spontaneous* enjoyment of work and capacity for love."[3] He felt that the repression of this deepest and benign layer of the human being brought forth the "Freudian unconscious" in which sadism, greediness, lasciviousness, envy, and

---

[2] Eric Berne, *Transactional Analysis in Psychotherapy* (New York: Grove Press, 1961).

[3] Wilhelm Reich, *The Function of the Orgasm* (New York: Farrar Straus and Giroux, Inc., 1961).

perversion of all kinds were regnant. Wilhelm Reich invented the term "sex economy" since he was interested in the economic analysis of the neuroses; according to this theory, sexual energy is manipulated for political reasons. The orgasm, the release of sexual energy, liberates a human system whose sexuality has been oppressed.

"The connection between sexual repression and the authoritarian social order was simple and direct: the child who experienced the suppression of his natural sexuality was permanently maimed in his character development; inevitably he became submissive, apprehensive of all authority and completely incapable of rebellion."[4] In other words, he developed exactly that character structure which would prevent him from seeking liberation. The first act of suppression prepared the way for every subsequent tyranny. Reich concluded that repression existed not for the sake of moral edification (as tradition religions would have it), nor for the sake of cultural development (as Freud claimed), but simply in order to create the character structure necessary for the preservation of a repressive society.

A great deal of Reich's writings were an attack against the patriarchal family which he saw as "a factory for authoritarian ideologies and conservative structures."[5] Reich felt that the authoritarian government and economic exploitation of the people were being maintained by the family and that the family was an indispensable part of it, which fulfilled its function as a supporter of exploitation by the oppression of sexuality in the young.

Herbert Marcuse is another writer who ties an economic point of view to the difficulties of mankind.

---

[4] P. A. Robinson, *The Freudian Left* (New York: Harper Colophon Books, 1969).

[5] Wilhelm Reich, *The Sexual Revolution* (New York: Noonday Press, 1962).

According to him, human beings are suffering alienation from themselves, their fellow human beings, and nature. This alienation is the result of a surplus repression superimposed on the repression that Freud postulated as necessary for the development of civilization. This surplus repression forces human beings to live according to the performance principle.

The performance principle is a way of life imposed on human beings which causes the desexualization of the body and the concentration of eroticism in certain bodily organs such as the mouth, the anus, and the genitals. This progression is not a healthy, biologically logical sequence, as Freudian theory sees it, but one that results in a reduction of human potential for pleasure. Concentrating pleasure into narrow erogenous zones leads to the production of a shallow, dehumanized, one-dimensional person. Marcuse feels that the concentration of sexual pleasure in the genitals is accomplished in order to free the rest of the body for the use by an oppressive establishment as an instrument of labor which can be exploited. "The normal progress to genitality has been organized in such a way that the partial impulses and their 'zones' were all but desexualized in order to conform to the requirements of a specific social organization of the human existence."[6]

Thus Marcuse and Wilhelm Reich connect the social and psychological manipulation of human beings by human beings surrounding them—including the family—with an oppressive social order. The following theory about the stroke economy is a similar effort in which it will be proposed that the free exchange of strokes, which is at one and the same time a human capacity, a human need, and a human right, has been artifically controlled for the purpose of rearing human beings who will behave in a way which is desirable to a larger

[6] Herbert Marcuse, *Eros and Civilization* (New York: Vintage Books, 1962).

social order. This manipulation of the stroke economy, unwittingly engaged in by the largest proportion of human beings, has never been understood as being a service to the established order, so that human beings have not had an opportunity to evaluate the extent to which such control of the stroke economy is to their own advantage and to what extent it is not.

In order to make this point more vivid, allow me to ask you to imagine that every human being was at birth fitted with a mask which controlled the amount of air that was available to him. This mask would at first be left wide open, allowing the child to breathe freely; but at the point at which the child was able to perform certain desired acts the mask would be gradually closed down and only opened at such times at which the child did whatever the grownups around it wanted it to do. Imagine, for instance, that a child was prohibited from manipulating his own air valve and that only other people would have control over it, and that the people allowed to control it would be rigorously specified. A situation of this sort could cause human beings to be quite responsive to the wishes and desires of those who had control over their air supply. If sanctions were made severe enough, people would not remove their masks even though the mask was quite easily removable, but would instead follow the prescriptions that regulated breathing of air.

Occasionally, some people would grow tired of their masks and take them off; but these people would be considered character disorder criminals, foolish, or reckless. People would be quite willing to do considerable work and expend much effort to guarantee a continuous flow of air. Those who did not work and expend such effort would be cut off, would not be permitted to breathe freely, and would not be given enough air to live in an adequate way.

People who openly advocated taking off the masks

would justifiably be accused of undermining the very fiber of the society which constructed these masks; for it would be very clear that as people removed them they would no longer work or be responsive to many of the demands that were placed upon them. Instead, these people would seek self-satisfying modes of life and relationships which could easily exclude a great deal of activity previously valued by a society based on the wearing of such masks. "Mask removers" would be seen as a threat to the society, and would probably be viciously dealt with. In an air-hungry society, air substitutes could be sold at high prices and individuals could, for a fee, sell clever circumventions of the anti-breathing rules.

Absurd as this situation may seem, I believe that it is a close analogy to the situation which exists presently among human beings in the area of strokes. Instead of a mask that controls the air, we have very strict regulations as to how strokes are exchanged. Children are controlled by regulating their stroke input, and grown-ups work and respond to societal demands to get strokes. The population is generally stroke-hungry and a large number of enterprises, such as massage parlors, Esalen, the American Tobacco Company, and General Motors, are engaged in selling strokes, or implying that their product will obtain strokes for their consumers ("ginger ale tastes like love").

Persons who defy the stroke-economy regulations are seen as social deviants, and if enough of them band together they are regarded as a threat to the National Security.

Most human beings live in a state of stroke deficit; that is, a situation in which they survive on a less-than-ideal diet of strokes. This stroke deficit can vary from mild to severe. An extreme example of a person's stroke starvation diet is the case of an alcoholic, by no means unique, who lived in a skid-row hotel. By his own account he received two strokes daily from the clerk at the hotel desk from Tuesday to Sunday and approximately thirty strokes on Monday when he appeared at the alcoholic clinic and exchanged strokes with the receptionist and the nurse administering medication. Once a month, he was treated to a dozen extra superstrokes from the physician who renewed his prescription. His vitality was almost completely sapped; he reminded me of human beings who live on starvation diets of rice. Eventually, his stroke-starved state of apathy prevented him from coming to the clinic and soon afterward he was found dead in his room.

Experiences of a person in such food- and stroke-starved circumstances are of a completely different order than the experiences of one who is properly fed. This man was little more than an automaton and certainly had nothing that could be interpreted as autonomy or self-determination. Most people, however, live in a less severe form of starvation leading to varying degrees of depression and agitation. People in these circumstances exhibit, instead of the apathy of the severely starved, a form of agitation or "search behavior," which is also found in the mildly food-starved person or animal.

Because people are forced to live in a state of stroke scarcity, the procurement of strokes fills every moment of their waking hours. This is the cause for structure hunger—that need to optimally structure time in social situations for the procurement of a maximum number of strokes. Just as in the case of money, certain people are able to obtain large numbers of strokes in return for little effort; that is, they have established a stroke monopoly in which they are able to accumulate others' strokes. In the stroke economy, just as is the case elsewhere, the rich get richer and the poor get poorer while the majority have to struggle daily to make ends meet.

The notion of stroke monopoly became clearly evident to me in connection with therapeutic marathons. A marathon, as I would conduct it, is in essence a temporary subculture with an anomalous stroke economy in which an attempt is made to disarm the injunctions that exist in people against stroking: "Don't give strokes." "Don't ask for strokes." "Don't accept strokes." "Don't reject strokes." Thus, a marathon is organized around the permission to ask and give as well as reject and accept strokes, so that the stroke economy can be said to be "free" and strokes are available in unlimited numbers. Such manipulation of the stroke economy profoundly affects the transactions between people. The group leader may remain outside the economy, not participating in the exchange of strokes, or he can participate in the stroke economy. If he does the latter, he will quickly find that he has an inordinate and unwitting control over the flow of strokes; he will be given strokes without having to ask and he will be able to give without being rejected. A therapist who enters into the economy and is unaware of this inordinate, monopolizing control which he has over the flow of strokes can be a disruptive factor nullifying his attempts at therapy.

Therapists, especially group therapists, are in a position to become stroke monopolists. Wyckoff (see Chapter 4) points out how men monopolize women's strokes. Parents are often interested in monopolizing their children's strokes. In every case, the stroke monopolist profits by the monopoly and at the same time perpetuates the general rules of the controlled stroke economy.

The free exchange of strokes between Child and Child is severely controlled by the Parent ego state on the basis of Parental tapes. These Parental tapes are easily demonstrable by a very simple technique called "bragging." If a person is asked to stand up in the middle of the room and brag—that is, make a number of self-praising statements—there would be an immediate response of reaction within that person's head. The person might feel that it would be immodest or improper to say good things about himself, or that to say good things about oneself might be seen as an insult to the others in the room.

Persons who accept the validity of bragging may find that they are not aware of good things about themselves, that they are incapable of using words which imply goodness or worth applied to themselves. If, at this point, other members of the group are asked to provide honest strokes, it often happens that the recipient of the strokes will systematically reject everything that is said with a Parental discount.

If someone says, "You have beautiful skin," the Parent says, internally, "They haven't seen you up close." If someone says, "You have a lovely smile," the Parent says, "But they haven't seen you cry." If someone says, "You have beautiful breasts," the Parent says, "That's all they think of you—you're just a sex object." If a person says, "You're very intelligent," then the Parent says, "Yes, but you're ugly." Other devices to avoid the acceptance of strokes will be observed, such as: giving token acceptance of the stroke, followed by a shrug so that the stroke will roll off the shoulders instead of soaking in; or an immediate reciprocation with a counter-stroke which essentially says, "I don't deserve the stroke so I must give one in return."

These Parental reactions to stroking are just those that occur in a situation of being given strokes, which is the simplest. In the situation of asking for strokes, it becomes even more complicated. There are all sorts of taboos operating which prevent the free exchange of strokes: the homosexual taboo that prevents stroking between men and men, and women and women; the heterosexual taboo that prevents stroking between men and women unless they are in a prescribed relationship, either engaged to be married or married; and the taboos against physical touch between grownups and children unless they are in a nuclear family, and then only under certain circumstances. In short, the free exchange of strokes is a managed activity, a situation in which the means for the satisfaction of people's needs are unavailable to them. The end result is that the most human of capacities, the capacity to love, is taken away from people, and then turned against them by using it as a means to bring about certain desired behavior.

It can be seen from this that a person or group of persons who free themselves from the strictures of the stroke economy will regain control of the means for the satisfaction of a most important need; consequently, they tend to disengage themselves from the larger society. It is because of this that there is such great panic among lawmakers and government officials in relation to the youth, drug, and sex culture. The notion that human beings will no longer work or be responsible when they liberate the stroke economy may be quite accurate if work and responsibility is seen as defined by others. However, it is quite another thing to assume that human beings in a free stroke economy will be as inert or vegetable-like as Freudian theory and the Judaeo-Christian view of humankind would predict. The notion that satisfied human beings will not work and will not be responsible has been a basic assumption of child-rearing. The facts may be quite different, however. It is my assumption that as they are satisfied in their stroke needs, human beings will be better able actually to pursue the achievement of harmony with themselves, others, and nature.

In my group work, the above stroke-economical understanding has caused me to shift some of my attention and emphasis to the issue of strokes. For instance, marital disharmony can be seen as part of a script, a game, or a pastime; but I have found that the key to its therapy is the freeing and equalizing of the exchange of strokes.

One couple's ten years of "Uproar," "Kick Me," and "Now I've Got You, You SOB" (NIGYSOB) came to a halt when a sharp focus on the exchange of strokes revealed that the husband was simply not interested in an equitable arrangement; he was neither willing to give more nor to ask less. This couple knew the games they played, but had only been capable of achieving social control for short periods. With this new understanding, the woman pressed for a separation.

Another couple found that their love for each other was being eroded by a combination of factors; the wife craved—but had no permission to ask for—certain nurturing strokes and resented her husband for not giving them without being asked. The husband, on the other hand, did not understand the kinds of strokes she needed and had no permission to give them. They clashed repeatedly with accusations of "You don't *really* love me" from her, and stubborn defensiveness from him ("You are too demanding"), ending in despair for both. Therapy centered on a minute transactional analysis of their struggle over this issue and finally focused on giving permission through role-playing: to the wife for asking directly for nurturing strokes, and to the husband for giving them.

One of the functions of games is the extortion of recognition or strokes when they are not freely given. A husbandless mother of four was able to halt a hellish daily stroke rip-off involving "Kick Me" and "NIGYSOB" with her children by establishing a systematic stroke-feeding schedule which satisfied all her children and even left her some time for herself.

Freeing up the stroke economy is most effective the more people that are involved. A therapy group provides a good context in which the free exchange of strokes can be practiced. But persons who are free of stroke injunctions need social contexts which have free stroke economies or they will be under pressure to conform to the societal stroke-economical rules.

In my experience, persons who, in group, free themselves in their stroking tend to form social subgroupings (e.g. couples, families, communes, etc.) which are unresponsive to the larger societal stroke-economic demands. In these groupings, knowledge of the theory of the stroke economy and of the Fuzzy Tale are useful in understanding and coping with the problems of maintaining a free stroke economy.

A FUZZY TALE[7]

Once upon a time, a long time ago, there lived two very happy people called Tim and Maggie with two children called John and Lucy. To understand how happy they were, you have to understand how things were in those days. You see, in those days, everyone was given at birth a small, soft, Fuzzy Bag. Anytime a person reached into this bag he was able to pull out a Warm Fuzzy. Warm Fuzzies were very much in demand because whenever somebody was given a Warm Fuzzy it made him feel warm and fuzzy all over. People who didn't get Warm Fuzzies regularly were in danger of developing a sickness in their back which caused them to shrivel up and die.

In those days it was very easy to get Warm Fuzzies. Anytime that somebody felt like it, he might walk up to you and say, "I'd like to have a Warm Fuzzy." You would then reach into your bag and pull out a Fuzzy the size of a little girl's hand. As soon as the Fuzzy saw the light of day it would smile and blossom into a large, shaggy,

[7] Copyright © 1969 by Claude Steiner. *Transactional Analysis Bulletin,* 9:36, October, 1969.

Warm Fuzzy. You then would lay it on the person's shoulder or head or lap and it would snuggle up and melt right against their skin and make them feel good all over. People were always asking each other for Warm Fuzzies, and since they were always given freely, getting enough of them was never a problem. There were always plenty to go around and as a consequence everyone was happy and felt warm and fuzzy most of the time.

One day a bad witch became angry because everyone was so happy and no one was buying her potions and salves. The witch was very clever and so she devised a very wicked plan. One beautiful morning she crept up to Tim while Maggie was playing with their daughter and whispered in his ear, "See here, Tim, look at all the Fuzzies that Maggie is giving to Lucy. You know, if she keeps it up, eventually she is going to run out and then there won't be any left for you."

Tim was astonished. He turned to the witch and said, "Do you mean to tell me that there isn't a Warm Fuzzy in our bag every time we reach into it?"

And the witch said, "No, absolutely not, and once you run out, that's it. You don't have any more." With this she flew away on her broom, laughing and cackling hysterically.

Tim took this to heart and began to notice every time Maggie gave up a Warm Fuzzy to somebody else. Eventually he got very worried and upset because he liked Maggie's Warm Fuzzies very much and did not want to give them up. He certainly did not think it was right for Maggie to be spending all her Warm Fuzzies on the children and on other people. He began to complain every time he saw Maggie giving a Warm Fuzzy to somebody else, and because Maggie liked him very much, she stopped giving Warm Fuzzies to other people as often, and reserved them for him.

The children watched this and soon began to get the

idea that it was wrong to give up Warm Fuzzies any time you were asked or felt like it. They too became very careful. They would watch their parents closely, and whenever they felt that one of their parents was giving too many Fuzzies to others, they also began to object. They began to feel worried whenever they gave away too many Warm Fuzzies. Even though they found a Warm Fuzzy every time they reached into their bag, they reached in less and less and became more and more stingy. Soon people began to notice the lack of Warm Fuzzies, and they began to feel less and less fuzzy. They began to shrivel up and occasionally, people would die from lack of Warm Fuzzies. More and more people went to the witch to buy her potions and salves even though they didn't seem to work.

Well, the situation was getting very serious indeed. The bad witch who had been watching all of this didn't really want the people to die so she devised a new plan. She gave everyone a bag that was very similar to the Fuzzy Bag except that this one was cold while the Fuzzy Bag was warm. Inside of the witch's bag were Cold Pricklies. These Cold Pricklies did not make people feel warm and fuzzy, but made them feel cold and prickly instead. But, they did prevent people's backs from shriveling up. So, from then on, every time somebody said, "I want a Warm Fuzzy," people who were worried about depleting their supply would say, "I can't give you a Warm Fuzzy, but would you like a Cold Prickly?" Sometimes, two people would walk up to each other, thinking they could get a Warm Fuzzy, but one or the other of them would change his mind and they would wind up giving each other Cold Pricklies. So, the end result was that while very few people were dying, a lot of people were still unhappy and feeling very cold and prickly.

The situation got very complicated because, since the coming of the witch, there were less and less Warm

Fuzzies around; so Warm Fuzzies, which used to be thought of as free as air, became extremely valuable. This caused people to do all sorts of things in order to obtain them. Before the witch had appeared, people used to gather in groups of three or four or five, never caring too much who was giving Warm Fuzzies to whom. After the coming of the witch, people began to pair off and to reserve all their Warm Fuzzies for each other exclusively. If ever one of the two persons forgot himself and gave a Warm Fuzzy to someone else, he would immediately feel guilty about it because he knew that his partner would probably resent the loss of a Warm Fuzzy. People who could not find a generous partner had to buy their Warm Fuzzies and had to work long hours to earn the money. Another thing which happened was that some people would take Cold Pricklies (which were limitless and freely available), coat them white and fluffy, and pass them on as Warm Fuzzies. These counterfeit Warm Fuzzies were really Plastic Fuzzies, and they caused additional difficulties. For instance, two people would get together and freely exchange Plastic Fuzzies, which presumably should make them feel good, but they came away feeling bad instead. Since they thought they had been exchanging Warm Fuzzies, people grew very confused about this, never realizing that their cold prickly feelings were really the result of the fact they had been given a lot of Plastic Fuzzies.

So the situation was very, very dismal and it all started because of the coming of the witch who made people believe that some day, when least expected, they might reach into their Warm Fuzzy Bag and find no more.

Not long ago, a young woman with big hips and born under the sign of Aquarius came to this unhappy land. She had not heard about the bad witch and was not worried about running out of Warm Fuzzies. She gave them out freely, even when not asked. They called her the Hip Woman and disapproved of her because she was giving the children the idea that they should not worry about running out of Warm Fuzzies. The children liked her very much because they felt good around her, and they began to give out Warm Fuzzies whenever they felt like it. The grownups became concerned and decided to pass a law to protect the children from depleting their supplies of Warm Fuzzies. The law made it a criminal offense to give out Warm Fuzzies in a reckless manner. The children, however, seemed not to care, and in spite of the law they continued to give each other Warm Fuzzies whenever they felt like it and always when asked. Because there were many many children, almost as many as grownups, it began to look as if maybe they would have their way.

As of now, it is hard to say what will happen. Will the grownup forces of law and order stop the recklessness of the children? Are the grownups going to join with the Hip Woman and the children in taking a chance that there will always be as many Warm Fuzzies as needed? Will they remember the days their children are trying to bring back when Warm Fuzzies were abundant because people gave them away freely?

4. WOMEN'S SCRIPTS AND THE STROKE ECONOMY by Hogie Wyckoff

Many of the women in group with me experience themselves as being in a stroke deficit. Strokes are positive human recognition which can be in the form of compliments, lovemaking, etc. There are several reasons for this, but I believe the primary one to be that women tend to give out more strokes than they receive. They are enjoined to do this by the dictates of their roles as women. The instruction to give more strokes than they receive and to be willing to settle for this disparity are essential aspects of women's life scripts.

A script is a life-plan decided upon at an early age. It is induced by certain powerful messages—injunctions (Don't) and attributes (Do)—which are transmitted by parents and society. In this chapter I am concerned with the everyday, garden variety of scripts known as banal scripts.[1] These do not necessarily lead to a tragic ending as do hamartic scripts but, rather, result in restrictions of autonomy and, in the case of women, allow exploitation of their stroking capacities.

Stroke exploitation is necessary because of the deficiencies created in men and women as a result of sex

[1] Claude Steiner, *Scripts People Live* (New York: Grove Press, 1974).

roles. Speaking in generalities, men are encouraged to develop their Adult capacities and function well as producers and performers. Women, on the other hand, are encouraged to develop their Nurturing Parent to use on others, to be loving wives and mothers, and function well as nurturers and supporters. Dot Vance[2] points out that the worst thing a man can be is impotent, unable to perform; and the worst thing a woman can be is frigid, unable to be warm.

Because of their role expectations, men often lose touch with their feelings and their warmth. They tend to be tuned out to other people's emotional needs, and thus lack the ability to be tuned in and to respond. Women are more in touch with their feelings and also have more permission to respond to the feelings of others. It is thus that sex roles turn human beings into one-dimensional specialists incapable of functioning autonomously. Because of this incompleteness, men and women tend to fit together much like halves of a whole; and, like puzzle pieces, mesh to fill each others' empty spaces. This is why a woman will often agree to enter into a relationship in which she provides most of the loving Nurturing Parent and strokes in return for monetary and security considerations. She and others consider her incapable in certain areas of Adult functioning and believe that safety and fulfillment can only be provided by someone else, specifically a man. This incompleteness has forced women and men to barter with strokes. Traditionally, women have been forced to use their capacity as stroke givers as a means of enticing a man into a marriage. They can thus barter with a man for emotional and economic security. Classically: "I won't sleep with you unless you marry me."

This bartering is also promoted by the stroke econ-

---

[2] Dot Vance, "Reclaiming Our Birthright—Getting It Together with Warmth and Potency," *Radical Therapist,* II, 3 (October, 1971).

omy, an artificial limit placed on strokes. It makes strokes into a commodity with object value rather than the free, unlimited expression of human affection that they can be. When being indoctrinated in our culture, we are told: "You may only stroke certain people at certain times under certain conditions." So people come to think of their stroking in terms of cultural limitations, making the situation one of artificial scarcity. Stroking tends to be seen as sexual, and people are cut off from each other's strokes unless they relate on this basis. Thus, men mustn't touch other men or they may be thought homosexual. Women have a little more permission to touch each other and this can easily be encouraged in women's groups, a very important first step in helping them to free themselves from their stroke hunger and disadvantageous barter agreements.

I am going to present some women's scripts in an effort to explicate how women are trained to accept the mystification that they are incomplete, inadequate, and dependent, and how this promotes them to embrace a situation of stroke exploitation. The fantasies women have about themselves as they grow up, life-plan expectations of being mothers and attractive sex objects, begin to be instilled into their every fiber the moment they are wrapped in pink rather than in blue, and are continually reinforced from that moment on by parents, schools, and peers. The media impinge upon women in constant, subtle ways, seductively backing all these messages. The sex-role stereotypes are not only urged on women by the media but are age-old, and are reflected, for instance, by goddesses in Greek mythology: Athene as a prototype of Woman Behind the Man; Hera as a Mother Hubbard; Aphrodite as Plastic Woman; and also by reifications in psychotherapy, such as the Anima and Animus archetypes in Jung.

The scripts I will describe are chosen for recognition value. They differ in many aspects but they all share one thing in common: they promote stroke exploitation of women. They illustrate how some women are programmed to blindly accept their role as stroke sources, giving more than they receive, often like stroke cows, bred to be "stupid" and willing to be consumed as members of an exploited and violated herd.

Women engage in stroke barter according to the guidelines of their scripts. In presenting them I will indicate the thesis or life plan and how it permits stroke usury, the injunctions and permissions or attributes, the counter-oppression, the therapist's role, and finally, the antithesis.

The therapist's role is that which supports the script and which the "patient" expects the therapist to play when she applies for treatment. The counter-oppression is included because it often is mistakenly pointed to as proof of women's oppression of men. Clearly, however, these two categories—men's oppression of women and women's oppression of men—are not comparable; the script specifies that women are to be secondary to men and/or their subjects, and the counter-oppression is an attempt at righting this inequity which, however, never completely succeeds. In this sense it is like the guerrilla warfare of the oppressed who may be quite successful in draining the energies of the oppressor but who are not able to get out from under.

MOTHER HUBBARD (OR WOMAN BEHIND THE FAMILY)

THESIS: She takes care of everyone but herself. She gives twenty strokes for every one that she gets and accepts this inequity because she feels she is the least important member of the family and that her worth is only as a source of supplies. This inequity is constantly made legitimate by the media's promotion of the role of "housewife and mother" as capable of providing women with meaning and fulfillment. She feels worthless because strokes and meaning in life do not come to her for herself and her labors, but for her "family"—husband and children. When her task and usefulness to others in life ends, often with menopause, she undergoes psychic death (involutional melancholia) and may be dealt a rude shock (ECT) in return for her life's labor.

INJUNCTIONS AND ATTRIBUTIONS:

Sacrifice for others
Be nice
Be a good: housewife/cook/mother

COUNTER-OPPRESSION: She refuses to make love to her husband, saying she's too busy or too tired, or by having a headache, with the hope that he will finally give her nurturing strokes in return.

THERAPIST'S ROLE: The therapist tells her not to get angry, gives her tranquilizers to keep her comfortable, and eventually finishes her off with electroshock therapy (ECT).

ANTITHESIS: She begins listening to and respecting her own inner desires; she starts getting strokes *for who she is* and *not for what she can give*. She starts demanding that people ask for what they want from her, and does not give more than she receives in return. It's essential that she begin to put herself and her needs before those of others.

Once it is under way, this script is difficult to overcome because of the bleakness of the alternatives available to, say, an unskilled mother of four. But women who really want to change can take power over their lives—they can fight to create their lives *the way they want them to be* and to cooperate with and get support from other women to do it. They can work and cooperate in raising their children together and in exchanging child care. Eventually, they can also fight together in action groups for improved day care and welfare rights.

WOMAN BEHIND THE MAN

THESIS: She puts all her talent and drive into supporting her husband who is often less talented than she is, but is "supposed" to be the successful one. She has no children, looks "smart" at cocktail parties, is a good hostess and campaign manager. She is a female Cyrano de Bergerac: the grey eminence who cannot shine because of a congenital defect (her sex) that makes her socially unacceptable in a position of leadership.

She gives her husband many strokes in an effort to be supportive and allows him to receive ones she's actually earned. For example, she ghost-writes most of her husband's book and *he* takes all the credit. She must be satisfied to glow in applause for *him*. She must not get upset or jealous when other women want to give him strokes because he's such a success.

This script can be the least exploitative when it provides some real recognition for the woman as "the woman behind the man."

INJUNCTIONS AND ATTRIBUTIONS:

Be helpful
Don't take credit
Stand behind your man

COUNTER-OPPRESSION: She might have an affair with a political opponent or sporadically break down in her role as "Girl Friday" in order to highlight her importance in his work.

THERAPIST'S ROLE: He reminds her of her limitations as a woman and of her duty to support her husband.

ANTITHESIS: The way out is for her to start taking credit for her talent and to use it in her own behalf. She must take the necessary risks and responsibility to be a success in her own right, on her own terms, and not cop out by being behind "him." She should be angry about past inequity and refuse to go along with it any longer. She can tell her husband to hire secretarial and editorial services and start doing her own work and taking credit for it.

PLASTIC WOMAN

THESIS: In an effort to obtain strokes, she encases herself in plastic: bright jewelry, platform heels, foxy clothes, intriguing perfumes, and dramatic make-up. She tries to buy beauty and O.K.-ness, but never really succeeds. When she loses her looks, she feels she's lost everything. After a certain point, superficial beauty can't be bought and pasted on, so she ends up depressed with no strokes that she values. She may then try to fill the void with alcohol, tranquilizers, or other chemicals.

She gives sexual strokes in return for money, but these don't satisfy her because she doesn't reach orgasm.

INJUNCTIONS AND ATTRIBUTIONS:

Money will get you what you want in life
Don't get old
Don't be yourself

COUNTER-OPPRESSION: She begins "beating" him to death with a plastic charge plate. (He has a heart attack keeping up with her charge accounts.) No return orgasm in sexual intercourse makes him doubt his ability as a lover. She uses her husband's money to buy strokes from an analyst.

THERAPIST'S ROLE: He prescribes drugs and engages her in an extended course of individual psychotherapy sessions. He decides that group psychotherapy is "not indicated" and sees her three or four times a week.

ANTITHESIS: She starts to like her natural self and decides not to settle for an unsatisfactory sex life. She concludes that her "power" as a consumer is an illusion and decides to reclaim power over her life by taking responsibility for creating it. She no longer takes drugs to blur out what's unsatisfactory about her life but, rather, joins a problem-solving group and learns how to make real changes. She works on developing aspects of herself other than her appearance that both she and others can appreciate. She begins to enjoy exercising and gets herself into a hiking club to meet new people. She commits herself to being concerned with how she feels on the inside rather than how she looks from the outside. She discards cosmetics and other plastic, unnatural junk.

POOR LITTLE ME

THESIS: Her parents do everything for her because she is a girl, thus debilitating her and making her completely dependent upon them and under their control. After she tries fighting against this she finally gives up and becomes a Victim looking for a Rescuer. She succeeds in this by marrying a "prominent man," often a doctor or psychiatrist who plays a rescuing Daddy to "his" helpless little girl. She gets no strokes for being an O.K. person and is kept not O.K. because she only gets supportive strokes when she's really down. The strokes she does get are thus bittersweet to her. He, on the other hand, gets strokes for being a good Daddy to a loser, sexual strokes in appreciation from her and, finally, strokes as a martyred husband when she totally falls apart.

INJUNCTIONS AND ATTRIBUTIONS:

Don't grow up
Do what your parents say
Don't think

COUNTER-OPPRESSION: She goes crazy, makes public scenes to embarrass him, and generally creates doubt in the community as to his competence as a man or therapist.

THERAPIST'S ROLE: He plays Rescuer, and when she relapses after a brief period of progress, he calls her "unmotivated" or schizophrenic and switches to Persecutor.

ANTITHESIS: She decides to be a responsible adult and take care of business for herself. She begins to get strokes for being O.K. and refuses to accept strokes for being a Victim. She knows those strokes collude with the self-destructive Pig in her to make her feel powerless. She starts developing her own physical and mental powers. She feels high on her own strength and health. She makes a commitment to herself to keep it that way.

CREEPING BEAUTY

THESIS: She has the standard attributes of "media beauty," yet she doesn't feel very good about herself as a human being and really doesn't believe that she's lovely. Rather, she thinks of herself as being shallow and ugly. When she looks in the mirror she does not see her beauty but only sees her blemishes and imperfections. People only seem to respond to her as a pretty face; and, because she's not treated as an equal or respected as an intelligent person, she decides to give up fighting and to "sell" herself as a sex object in order to get what she wants from others. However, she believes she's deceiving everyone who thinks she's beautiful and believes people who buy that deception are fools, anyway.

She gets strokes for being beautiful but discounts them. She really wants to be liked as a person but no one is willing to see past her exterior beauty. She ends up giving sexual strokes, but not receiving any acceptable strokes in return. Any man with her gets strokes for having such a lovely "possession."

INJUNCTIONS AND ATTRIBUTIONS:

Be lovely on the outside
You're not O.K.
Don't be close to people

COUNTER-OPPRESSION: Getting men to come across with as much as they will and then not delivering the goods (herself).

THERAPIST'S ROLE: He becomes sexually aroused by her and propositions her. She then concludes he is just like all the rest.

ANTITHESIS: She must demand strokes for qualities people appreciate in her other than her beauty and refuse to accept strokes for only her physical appearance. She can then begin to like herself and begin to enjoy her true inner and outer beauty. She can do things that are meaningful to her and learn how to cooperate in a women's problem-solving group to get what she wants.

Strokes are essential to human life, and adequate stroking is essential to well-being. Women's scripts, by promoting a constant stroke deficit in women, are the sources of much difficulty and unhappiness.

One way for women to overcome these inhibiting and self-defeating scripts is to work on their problems in a women's problem-solving group. There women discuss problems and develop a subtle awareness of how various forms of oppression, particularly sex role definitions and expectations, affect them. While gaining this awareness a woman is given permission to transact with others in new ways and learn to assert her equality to men. The group provides her with protection and support as she makes the changes she desires, as well as supplying her honest strokes, thus decreasing her chronic stroke-hunger and making her less likely to accept inequitable barter agreements.

Ultimately, however, the way to eliminate sex role scripting is by telling children that they are complete, whole human beings and not indoctrinating them into the sex role ideology.

A woman who frees herself of a banal script would be free not to accept unequal situations. She wouldn't be an incomplete person bartering for safety. She would be able to avoid being stuck in unhappy relationships. She would be open to a greater variety of stroking relationships and be able to choose freely what's best for herself.

5. TEACHING RADICAL PSYCHIATRY

by Claude Steiner

Radical psychiatry has as one of its goals the demystification of human activities. The growing awareness that the process of schooling is the most fundamental and thoroughgoing means of mystification and therefore ultimately of oppression of people in our society and that schools are fundamentally low-security, correctional institutions has compelled many to completely reject the official forms of professional education and set out to search for reasonable alternatives to it.

Radical psychiatry was first taught at the Free University in Berkeley, one such alternative project of education. The Free University is an enormously successful institution which is practically indestructible and which serves large numbers of people through the simplest skeleton operation. The theoretical principles guiding the Free University are vague, primarily counter-instituional, and its functioning mostly pragmatic. The purpose of this chapter is to outline a similar educational system expressly for the purpose of teaching psychiatry.

In the development of this system I am greatly indebted to Ivan Illich whose ideas on de-schooling are the foundation on this paper.[1]

[1] Ivan Illich, "Schools Must Be Abolished," *The New York Review of Books*, XV, 1 (July 2, 1970). Also, Ivan Illich, "A

Psychiatry is probably the most vivid modern-day example of the manner in which ordinary schooling mystifies and makes unavailable to people their own most important resources. "Rich and poor alike depend on schools and hospitals which guide their lives, form their world view, and define for them what is legitimate and what is not. Both view doctoring oneself as irresponsible, learning on one's own as unreliable, and community organization, when not paid by those in authority, as a form of aggression or subversion."[2]

The "knowledge" which is part of psychiatric training is without a doubt the most complex, mystified system of half-truths and irrelevancies ever taught as a body of knowledge, approached in its absurdity only by its cousin, phrenology. No one in the field of psychiatry takes more than a small segment of it seriously, and every part of what is taught in psychiatry is fundamentally questioned by some sector of the profession. No parallel to this type of a situation exists in any other form of professional training, although it closely parallels the situation existing in medicine when medicine usurped the practice of psychiatry during the nineteenth century.

For instance, in psychiatry the student is taught psychoanalytic theory on the one hand, and psychopharmacology on the other. Yet, in almost every case, those who believe in psychoanalytic theory will reject psychopharmacological knowledge, and vice versa. The same is true concerning any number of other subcategories: individual psychotherapy versus group psychotherapy, Freudian theory versus neo-Freudian theory, and so on. Practicing psychiatrists are forced to reject as useless the majority of what they are taught as psychiatric knowledge in their schooling, even though they

---

New System of Education Without Schools," *The New York Review of Books,* XV, 12 (January 7, 1971).

[2] *Ibid.,* "Schools Must Be Abolished."

may continue to teach it to others. As psychiatrists are produced by the high institutions of learning they are all represented as being equally competent and equally knowledgeable in what is thought to be an accurate, valid, and reliable science by those who practice it, and the few who are its consumers. The fact that the largest majority of the public rejects psychiatry as having no validity for themselves, and that the largest portion of the medical profession is quite skeptical of it, on the other hand, is seen as a form of perversion of thinking or understanding rather than as a valid criticism of the profession.

This situation finds no parallel in any other science. Imagine, for instance, a physicist questioning in her thinking half of what she learned in her training, so that no group of physicists could be found to agree on more than a minute portion of their theoretical beliefs. Such a state of affairs would truly invalidate them as scientists or as useful, pragmatic professionals. Yet, psychiatry, through the mystification of the complexity and usefulness of psychiatric knowledge, continues to maintain incredibly powerful holds on the well-being of people; psychiatrists are seen as experts on human behavior even though it is impossible to get any agreement between them except that which comes from propinquity (schoolmates, officemates, businessmates); and psychiatry continues to be taught, at incredibly high expense, to a few chosen ones who can master the hurdles of "higher education" who then will, in the tradition of the medical profession in the United States, see themselves as justified in extracting high incomes from its practice.

TEACHING RADICAL PSYCHIATRY

Experiences of teaching radical psychiatry at the Berkeley Rap Center have brought to light certain problems which have their roots in the assumptions inherent in the schooling of persons wishing training as well as those providing training. People seeking training had a passive, somewhat resentful, and consumer-like attitude about what they were learning; they approached the teachings in radical psychiatry much in the same way as the student approaches courses at the university. Because these courses are forced on them and because they have no control over their destiny in the institution, students are generally resentful of being students and express their resentment through garrulousness about what is being taught and through an attitude of passive consumerism much like that of a person who sits in front of a television set, turns it on, complains about the quality of the programming throughout the viewing, and then shuts the television off and forgets everything except the vaguest outlines of what he has viewed. This attitude is matched by the teachers who, because they are not generally teaching what they know best or what they are most interested in, and because they realize that what they are teaching is being forced on the students, are willing to take a rather benign, liberal attitude about their teaching which allows for the expression of hostility in the form of theoretical debate. This attitude is similar to the attitude of a parent feeding a child spinach or some other "good" but bad-tasting food and indulgently allowing the child to complain and make a minor mess while doing so.

These attitudes were found to be a great problem at the Berkeley Rap Center. People would hear that there was a training program in radical psychiatry; they would attend; they would sit and listen to what teachers had to say; they would argue some small point and/or eventually discount or criticize all of the teachings. Teachers, on the other hand, would make themselves responsible for a curriculum and were willing to engage in interminable arguments, many of which were perverse forms of discounting on the part of the students, and generally wear themselves out in what seemed a fruitless attempt to train competent psychiatrists. In time the training program was filled with an excess of people, many of whom were resentful of the teachers whom they saw as withholding information from them, and expressed their resentment by constant questioning of basic principles and tenets, while at the same time withdrawing the work or individual effort which was required to maintain the operation of the Rap Center. The teachers, on the other hand, saw themselves as beleaguered, not appreciated, resentful of the trainees, and guilty about withholding from individuals the loving and devoted teaching which they felt a teacher should offer students.

At the new Radical Psychiatry Center (1970):

1. Persons wishing to be trained as radical psychiatrists should be made aware of the fact that what we are offering is a situation where people can learn to do what we are doing. As a consequence, our principal activity will be to teach and demonstrate our skills, rather than to debate or demonstrate their validity. Thus, a person entering the training program will stay in the program as long as she feels that what we're doing is something that she wants to participate in. The purpose of the program is not to proselytize or to convince people who do not believe what we believe in; therefore the discussions in the training situation will primarily be discussions of what we are doing, and what we believe will be explained rather than justified. This could be misinterpreted to mean that we don't welcome criticism. In fact, we feel criticism is essential, about *how* we teach from our trainees, but about *what* we teach only from those we feel have understood and used it.

People entering the program will be given some of the basic readings which, together with what they may have observed in the way of psychiatric activity in the contact rap and otherwise, will give them an idea of whether they want to participate in the program. If, as they get deeper into the material, they find that it is antithetical to their point of view, or that they do not want to participate in it, they should not try to stay in it. This model is similar to the craftsman-apprentice training situation where the apprentice is allowed to work in close proximity with the craftsman. In a situation of this sort, an apprentice will be able to make observations and suggestions which a good craftswoman will take into consideration and accept or reject as she sees fit. However, the apprentice is at no point under the illusion that he can change the craft fundamentally until he himself has become a craftsman. Teaching is a labor of love, and a person should not have to teach or learn from one with whom she does not have positive rapport any more than she would make love to such a person.

2. The training at the Radical Psychiatry Center will be given for and in the context of work at the Radical Psychiatry Center. Radical psychiatry depends for its functioning on people who are not learning simply for the purpose of acquiring knowledge that can be catalogued alongside other forms of knowledge. Such people are not acceptable in a program of this sort because they will not produce work for the community. People who want to learn radical psychiatry for use in other communities may do so, but must demonstrate their interest in work by working at the Radical Psychiatry Center during their apprenticeship. Work, or the performance in the service of psychiatry, will be the only criterion whereby a person's advancement in the training program should be judged. Neither professional degrees nor any other mystified performances such as utterances at meetings or promises of services to be performed in the future should be allowed to have any decision-making power in the running or the adminis-

tration of the Radical Psychiatry Center's activities; and the extent of a person's influence in the workings of the Radical Psychiatry Center should depend only on the extent of their work.

Work can be of two basic forms: direct service to the incoming public at the Contact rap or Heavy rap groups; and the training of radical psychiatrists. The responsibility of training is assumed not only by teaching one's skills but also by being an active participant in the peer groups; that is to say, by replacing the usual student's passivity with an active commitment and interest in the subject matter and its understanding so that a person's training responsibilities begin on their first day of training.

According to Ivan Illich, an educational system or network which adequately replaces the present schooling situation includes the following three purposes: "It should provide all who want to learn with access to available resources at any time in their lives; empower all who want to share what they know to find those who want to learn it from them; and, finally, furnish all who want to present an issue to the public with an opportunity to make their challenge known. . . . I believe that no more than four, possibly even three, distinct 'channels' or learning exchanges could contain all the resources needed for real learning."[3]

Illich's concern is primarily with the education of children, but what he says about children can be applied almost in its entirety to the education of radical psychiatrists. "The child grows up in a world of things, surrounded by people who serve as models for skills and values. He finds peers who challenge him to argue, to compete, to cooperate, and to understand; and if the child is lucky he is exposed to confrontation or criticism by an experienced elder who really cares. Things, models, peers, and elders are four resources each of

[3] *Ibid.*, "A New System of Education Without Schools."

which requires a different type of arrangement to insure that everybody has ample access to them."

These four resources—things, models, peers, and elders—are of great relevance in the training of psychiatrists, and I will postulate a training program which is based on them. Illich uses the word "network" to designate specific ways to provide access to each of the four sets of resources. The radical psychiatry training program should provide four such networks: a network of educational objects; a network of skill exchange; a network of peers; and a network of elders.

EDUCATIONAL OBJECTS

The principal educational objects of radical psychiatry are freely available and accessible to the student; namely, other human beings.

One of the mystifications of psychiatry is that human beings are not easily observable or understandable, and that it takes a greatly trained eye to understand their behavior. Illich points out how "industry has surrounded people with artifacts whose inner works only specialists are allowed to understand. The non-specialist is discouraged from figuring out what makes a watch tick or a telephone ring or an electric typewriter work by being warned that it will break if he tries. He can be told what makes a transistor radio work, but he cannot find out for himself. This type of design tends to reinforce a non-inventive society in which the experts find it progressively easier to hide behind their expertise and beyond evaluation."

The problem presented by Illich in regard to the way in which industry mystifies the working of its products can be extended to psychiatry, which mystifies the workings of its materials so as to make it impossible for people to feel that they are able to manipulate and work with other people and so as to cause them to be afraid that if they do they will cause irreparable harm. This also makes it possible for psychiatrists to hide behind their expertise so as to remain beyond questioning. Remaining beyond questioning is especially important to the psychiatrist because of his sense that his knowledge is not really scientific or valid.

While the objects of study in radical psychiatry are freely available in the streets and where everyone goes, certain settings are more conducive to understanding the basic structure of human beings. The Contact rap, as an instance, is such a place in which human beings are more likely to expose themselves openly to the scrutiny of other human beings for the purpose of being understood and understanding others. People who come to the Contact rap may, if they are in dire psychiatric distress, expose themselves freely. Others may wish to engage in psychiatric games or exercises which make the inner workings of the human being more readily available and open to scrutiny by others. Games such as "Bragging," "Trashing the Stroke Economy," or "Offing the Pig," games specifically designed for the study of radical psychiatry, are good mediums for making the objects of study available to the student in the Contact rap.

The most fundamental phenomenon to be observed in the study of radical psychiatry is alienation. Alienation can be observed under many guises: the alienation of a person who is listening to a conversation without participating; or the alienation of a person who has become the focus of a whole group's attention; or the alienation of a teacher who finds himself unable to satisfy his class; or the alienation of a man from his body in the form of drug abuse; or the alienation of women and men due to male chauvinism; or the alienation of persons from their own experiences are all readily observable phenomena of interest to the student of radical psychiatry. The deductions about the mystifications that veil the oppression that causes the alienation are, of course, of encompassing interest to the radical psychiatrist. Materials for the study of this data are readily available and at the disposal of anyone at any time he wishes to study them.

Writings are the other class of educational objects essential in radical psychiatry, and can be roughly divided into principles and techniques.

Radical psychiatry includes certain principles which are seen as essential to it and which are therefore accepted by radical psychiatrists a priori. They are:

1. *That psychiatry is a political activity.*

2. *That psychiatric difficulties are forms of alienation which is the result of mystified oppression, so that the activity of psychiatry is to seek liberation which is achieved through contact and awareness.* The rest of the writings in radical psychiatry are descriptions of techniques which define the state of the art at this point in time in the context of the Berkeley Radical Psychiatry Center. They involve group leadership skills, transactional analysis theory, gestalt techniques, and a series of other tools, gleaned from other modern psychiatric technology and developed by radical psychiatrists. This body of technique is highly flexible, and it is expected that it will change as contexts change and as better tools are developed.

The above description excludes as *essential* educational objects all other writings in psychiatry. This exclusion is a deliberate attempt to demystify the knowledge in a field which is overwhelmed with irrelevant writings.

The demystification of educational objects becomes more difficult as one teaches persons with "higher" levels of education. Postgraduates tend to see lectures, turgid writings, and persons with "higher" degrees as the most desirable sources of education. High school dropouts, on the other hand, know that neither lectures, degrees, nor most writings have much relevance to their lives and have a healthy disrespect for them. As a consequence, it is much easier to train a talented high school dropout of a certain age than it is to train an equally talented graduate of the same age. The rule of thumb in this respect is: "It takes five years to train a radical psychiatrist, except that it takes an extra year for every year of graduate training the person has had." This is because much of what is involved in training radical psychiatrists is deschooling or unlearning of mystifications.

The perversion of people's capacities due to "higher" education finds specific manifestations in reading and writing. A good college student is likely to have been severely damaged as a writer; graduate students especially are trained to write about things that interest no one in a way that no one would want to read—which is understandable since professors have a vested interest in not allowing any writing that is more readable than their own. Reading is likewise damaged: college students are burdened by a sense of guilt about all that they have not read, so that pleasurable reading is prohibited until the "required" reading is done. The result is that a reading phobia develops and no reading at all takes place. This is the desired end result of our educational system; namely, that no meaningful writing or reading be done by the educated. One of the tasks of radical psychiatry is to reunite people with their alienated capacities for communicating through the written word; we accomplish it through demystification of writings and through a writers' group in which writings in radical psychiatry are discussed and encouraged.

SKILL EXCHANGES

The practice of radical psychiatry requires certain undeniable skills. These skills, while quite definite and quite important, are, on the other hand, relatively easy to transmit to most people who are inclined to learn them. The skills of psychiatry have been widely mystified to such a point that most people feel incapable of performing or learning them.

"A 'skill model' is a person who possesses a skill and is willing to demonstrate its practice. A demonstration of this kind is frequently a necessary resource for a potential learner. . . . For most widely shared skills a person who demonstrates the skill is the only human resource we ever need or get. . . . A well motivated student who does not labor under a specific handicap often needs no further human assistance than can be provided by someone who can demonstrate on demand how to do what the learner wants to do. . . . What makes skills scarce on the present educational market is the institutional requirement that those who can demonstrate them may not do so unless they are given public trust through its certificate. . . . Converging self-interests now conspire to stop man from sharing his skills. The man who has the skill profits from its scarcity and not from its reproduction. The teacher who specializes in transmitting the skill profits from the artisan's unwillingness to launch his own apprentice into the field."[4]

These quotes from Ivan Illich concerning the nature of skill exchanges suggest how the radical psychiatry "skill models" should be made available to students. These skill models need only be individuals who have demonstrated a certain level of skill. They need not be in any way diagnosticians of learning difficulties or motivators, but simply individuals who know how to do a certain thing. When students convene with these skill teachers it should be made clear to them that the skill teachers'

---

[4] *Ibid.*

only responsibility is to demonstrate their skill and not to be good teachers, inspiring lecturers, or brilliant demonstrators. This can be explained in terms of an anti-consumerism stance which places in the student as much burden for learning as it does on the skill model. The only "teaching skill" needed by the skill model outside of his skill as a radical psychiatrist is the ability to convey to the learner the above participatory attitude which has often been squelched in people. Skills should be taught in small groups of no more than ten to make a participatory attitude possible.

PEER MATCHING

The concept of peer matching is perhaps the most revolutionary concept of Ivan Illich's. It involves getting together two or more people who have simply identified themselves by name and address and have described the activity in which they seek a peer. This approach, unpretentious and simple-minded as it may seem, has the great advantage of creating groups of people around their self-chosen and motivated interest. The only possible disadvantage or drawback of such a coalition of people is that their stated interest may not match their real interest, as is often the case when people appear to coalesce around a certain subject matter when in fact they are coalescing around interest in stroking or human contact. This difficulty can be dealt with by making human contact groups one of the possible categories for peer matching. In any case, this type of peer matching should be a part of radical psychiatry training. It dovetails with the skill exchange level in that a certain peer-matched group may choose to coalesce around a certain skill model to learn certain skills.

ELDERS

After having been liberated from the authoritarian structure and the consumer attitudes of the university setting, people's willingness to seek leadership will tend to increase. The same effect will be observed with respect to people's willingness to return to reading relevant writings. "We may expect that they will experience more deeply both their own independence and the need for guidance. . . . As they are liberated from manipulation by others they learn to profit from the discipline others have acquired in a lifetime. . . . As teachers abandon their claim to be superior informants or skill models, their claim to superior wisdom will begin to ring true."[5]

This is essentially an argument for the validity and value of the expertise of elders. The relationship of an elder to a student is that of a skilled craftsman to an apprentice. "What is common to all true master-pupil relationships is the awareness both share that the relationship is literally priceless—and in very different ways a privilege for both. . . . Aristotle speaks of it as a 'moral type of relationship, which is not on fixed terms; it makes a gift or does whatever it does as to a friend.' . . . Thomas Aquinas says of this kind of teaching that inevitably it is an act of love and mercy. This kind of teaching is always a luxury for the teacher and a form of leisure for him and his pupil: an activity meaningful for both having no ulterior purpose."[6]

Ivan Illich here vividly describes the sense that has become so urgent in radical psychiatry about the leveling of leadership and hierarchies. One of the difficulties encountered in teaching radical psychiatry is the criti-

---

[5] *Ibid.*

[6] *Ibid.*

cism encountered by "levelers" or "prison guards" in the Movement.[7] The criticism runs roughly as follows: "One of the greatest evils of all are oppressive hierarchies. All hierarchical structures must be abolished. Anyone pretending to have an expertise or presenting himself as a teacher is allowing the germ of an ultimately oppressive hierarchy to take root. This must be avoided and hierarchies must be uprooted as they begin developing." The result of this attitude when it takes hold in any kind of a training situation is to invalidate the knowledge and expertise of elders, and it is a mystified form of oppression where people are prevented from engaging in the transmission of knowledge. Elders are not designated or appointed, but simply are people whom others recognize as being especially knowledgeable or skillful. The elder-student coalitions can't be planned or pre-designed—they simply develop in any close working situation. They should, however, be encouraged by recognizing them for what they are; namely, one of the most rewarding and worthwhile of human relationships.

PRACTICE

On the basis of these principles a radical psychiatry training program would include:

1. An orientation to the materials.
    a. Contact rap.
    b. A guidebook describing contexts in which alienation can be studied.

2. A list of skill teachers who will make themselves available to groups of ten or less to demonstrate their skills.

[7] See Chapter 15, "Radical Psychiatry and Movement Groups," for a description of leveling and "Lefter Than Thou."

3. Written skill descriptions as skills are developed and made specific.

4. A mechanism (bulletin board with suggestions) for peer-group matching.

5. Working *elders* who are willing to establish learning relationships.

Section III
Therapy

6. CONTRACTUAL PROBLEM-SOLVING GROUPS by Claude Steiner

The bulk of the work of radical psychiatry goes on in contractual problem-solving groups. Such a group is composed of between eight and twelve persons who see themselves as having a problem, one or two trained radical psychiatrists who are capable of being helpful in solving such problems, and one or two observers who are trainees in the process of becoming radical psychiatrists. The group meets between two and three hours so as to provide each person with at least fifteen minutes of time at least once weekly. The group may be a men's group or a women's group or a mixed group, but there is no further attempt to select the persons who might be "suitable" for such a group; anyone stating that he or she has a problem and who seems willing to work on her or his problem in the context of the group is acceptable.

THE CONTRACT

All the persons in a group are bound by a contract. Drawing up a contract is the indispensable first step of the work in group.

A working contract is an agreement between the person seeking help and the group, including (especially) the group leader. The person seeking help should state what problem he or she has and how they desire the problem to be improved, in specific, behavioral, observable terms. This may include such wishes as finding a loved one, not being depressed, getting along with people, stopping drug abuse, or getting over being crazy. On the other hand, such wishes as self-understanding, emotional maturity, responsibility, or other such vague achievements sometimes expressed as the desired effect of group cannot be used in a contract because these terms aren't clear enough and are non-specific. It is not possible to enter into a contract on the basis of such vague goals; and, generally speaking, the best contracts are phrased in short sentences made up of short words understandable to an eight-year-old. In order for a contract to satisfy the requirements of mutual consent, it is necessary that all parties are able to specify to what they are consenting. The contract should therefore contain a clear description of what the person wants, what the group will offer, and the conditions which we consider to constitute the fulfillment of the contract.

The basic transactions of mutual consent are: 1) a request for help; 2) an offer of help; and 3) an acceptance of help. It is not unusual for a person to enter a therapeutic group without having achieved one or more of the above conditions. When a person enters group without requesting help, it is very unlikely that any work will be achieved. On the other hand, if a person requests help but the group leader or group members do not commit themselves to helping, it is likely that the person will be discounted. Finally, a group will usually include certain conditions to be fulfilled by the person seeking help, such as regular attendance, doing homework, and any number of other requests that imply acquiescence to the group culture; and a person requesting help who does not accept these conditions will also probably not get any work done. Thus, a clear acceptance of the offer to help is needed.

A person may, at the initial group meeting, not be able to precisely state what it is they want help with. However, this is usually because of people's reluctance, due to psychiatric mystification, to examine their situation in a simple-minded and straightforward way. When the question, "What are you unhappy with?" is asked, it is almost always possible to get a simple, straightforward answer which will ordinarily reveal some form of alienation, such as "I feel I am no good," "I am very depressed," "I can't make friends," "I cannot meet a lover," "I am addicted to drugs," "I can't think," "I am afraid all the time," "I can't get an erection," and so on. When problems are stated in this simple manner, it is equally simple to formulate a state of affairs which implies that the problem is solved and to enter into a mutual agreement to work on the problem.

A contract protects both the person who has a problem and the persons who want to help. The person who has the problem is able to delineate precisely where she or he wants help, and what needs to be changed, thereby avoiding having other people's value judgments as to what changes are needed or how they should live, imposed on him. On the other hand, the helpers are not drawn into a vague and nondescript plea for a Rescue.

THE GROUP WORK

The proceedings of a group can take two major divergent courses. On the one hand, the group can engage in work; or on the other it can engage in games.

Work

A group that engages in work follows approximately the following pattern: either by his own choosing or by being singled out by someone else, one group member will become the center of attention. This does not necessarily mean that he will be placed on the "hot seat" where he will become the *focus* of all interaction, but simply that he tends to be at the center of it. The first phase of this process is one of *clarification*. The person presents a problem, or someone else suggests that a problem exists, and some exploration is needed to ascertain whether there is in reality something to work on. The problem suggested by the person may be a "red herring" or a "bone" thrown at the group to distract it from a more serious problem. Or the problem, if suggested by another group member, may represent a projection or misperception. In any case, the process of clarification continues until the feeling develops that the group is working on a real problem area in which some change can or should occur. At this point the clarification gives way to *challenge*, and someone will ask overtly or covertly, "Now that we know the problem, what are you going to do about it?" The person ordinarily is at a loss for a solution or unwilling to use those which are suggested. A cherished old pattern of behavior is being examined and the person is expected to balk. This is the *impasse*. The group leader or someone else in the group proposes a certain course of action. This course of action is ordinarily one which the person has not used because of fear or uncertainty, and therefore the group and leader may have to apply some pressure. This pressure is consistent with the terms of the contract, and at this point the process shifts from *impasse* to *climax* if the person accepts the group's proposal, or to *anti-climax* if he deflects it. If the proposal is accepted, the group members will ordinarily have an experience of satisfaction and closure, and a silence will follow, after which the process starts over with another person as the focus of attention. If the person deflects the proposal, the leader is faced with a question of strategy. Should the work continue on the person or should the group give up and go on to someone else? This is probably the most crucial decision that a group leader must make. The leader who is under time pressure has the dual responsibility of not allowing time to be wasted and of pursuing matters to their completion. Skillful decisions along these lines distinguish the experienced group leader from the novice who will either pursue matters endlessly to no avail or drop them just as the impasse is ready to be broken.

Games

It takes a skillful leader to maintain the work orientation of a group. When a group loses its work orientation it will fall into game playing. Game playing can take several forms. The group can play Rescue in a situation where one of the persons presents himself as a Victim and the rest of the group scramble madly in their attempt to rescue. A group of this sort will be taken up by games such as "Why Don't You?—Yes, But," "Do Me Something," "If It Weren't For Them (or Him) (or Her)." The general outcome of such groups is that the Victim and Rescuers all end up in a state of heightened frustration and anger. Very often when a group has played a Rescue game the Rescuers will switch to Persecutors and now mercilessly attack the Victim. Now the games will be "Uproar," "Kick Me," "Now I've Got You, You Son Of A Bitch," "Stupid," and so on. Or the Victim becomes Persecutor and plays "Nobody Loves Me" or "See What You Made Me Do." The game roles of Victim, Rescuer, and Persecutor will switch around in the group with different people taking different roles so that everyone eventually plays every role in an endless merry-go-round.

The role of Rescuer is the natural game role that group leaders tend to fall into; and it is believed in radical psychiatry that for every long minute that a leader plays Rescuer, she or he will eventually have to play an equally long minute as Persecutor. The playing of Rescue is basically a situation in which the person is no longer honestly asking for the leader's help or is no longer willing to work in order to improve her situation. Another way of stating this is to say that when the leader or the group members are doing more than 50% of the work on a person's problem, a game of Rescue is taking place.

A group leader must be alerted to the possibility that a group member may no longer be holding to the contract, and when noticing that this is the case must call for the proceedings to come to a halt. The tendency for group leaders to engage in rescuing usually comes out of a sense of guilt or exaggerated responsibility for the group member. When a group leader maintains a position of "I'll help you as long as you are willing to work on your problem as hard as I do and not one second longer," she will avoid the dangers of the Rescue role. Needless to say, Persecuting any one person in a group is even less desirable than playing Rescue. In radical psychiatry we have concluded that problem-solving can be achieved without any necessity of "pigging" or the use of the Critical Parent. Yelling, screaming, attacking, goading, and other "therapeutic" maneuvers introduced into group work by Synanon are found to be unnecessary when a leader learns how to confront people in a human and loving way. Therefore, persecution is not allowed in radical psychiatry groups, especially not under the guise of "I'm Only Trying To Help You."

The view in radical psychiatry is that people who need psychiatric help are alienated and therefore the victims of mystified oppression. Thus, the correct response to a person who presents himself as a Victim is one of unconditional protection, understanding, and support. Given this support, the process of clarification in group will deal with what the person can do to remove the oppression and/or the mystifications that cause his alienation. It is at this point that a person may prefer to continue to be a Victim to moving against her oppression, at which time she is clearly in violation of her contract. The person who insists on being a Victim is not rejected or ostracized, but is simply made to see that his participation in a contractual problem-solving group is contradictory with his behavior, and that, for the moment at least, work on his problem can no longer continue.

7. PROBLEM-SOLVING GROUPS FOR WOMEN by Hogie Wyckoff

Because women as a class are grossly and subtly oppressed, while being mystified about this oppression, the majority of people who seek psychiatric help are women. Women are denied full access to their power as human beings; and, rather than expressing righteous anger about this violation, they regretfully come to view themselves and each other as being somehow deficient. Under the stress of this robbery and mind-rape, women break down more often than men. Due to sex role progamming, women have more permission than men do to be in touch with and admit their need for psychiatric help. The problem with this is that most of the "help" women receive is from psychiatrists whose values are ultimately anti-liberal and anti-women's liberation. At this point in history we as radical feminist psychiatrists believe that men, particularly professional, elitist, and sexist men, cannot help free women.

We *can* and *must* free ourselves. We can effectively take care of our own heads and souls. We can have the means of producing and preserving our own mental health. As oppressed people accustomed to adapting and compromising ourselves to the desires of others, scrupulously trained to tune in to other people's feelings, to second-guess, and to take care of their unspoken needs, we have already well-developed skills in intuition and insight. When these skills are coupled with permission and training to be strong, to take care of business, to think rationally, and to talk straight, the result is a skillful and powerful people's psychiatrist. For some time now, women in Berkeley have taken possession of the means of reclaiming their own mental well-being. Women who have themselves worked in women's problem-solving groups are learning to facilitate women's groups in training collectives.

The problem-solving group model has been developed, based on a synthesis of psychiatric theories taken from Eric Berne, R. D. Laing, and Claude Steiner, among others. Radical psychiatry's practice incorporates some basic tools of Eric Berne's transactional analysis.[1]

HOW THE GROUPS WORK

The basic structure is a group of eight women with one or two leaders which meets once a week for two hours. To facilitate the work a *contract* is used. This is a work agreement with the whole group, and in it each group member states simply and clearly what she would like to work on. The desired goal must involve some observable behavioral change. This is a vital element of a contract, since if there is no overt behavioral change desired there is no way for the group to be certain that the contract has been fulfilled. The contract guards the facilitator against imposing her values on the group member and allows them to decide if they can work with each other. If they can't both agree on a contract, they won't be able to work productively together. The contract keeps the emphasis on work in the "here and

[1] Eric Berne, *Principles of Group Treatment* (New York: Oxford University Press, 1966).

now" and provides a means for stimulating a person to work on her problem. It protects the group member from being manipulated by the facilitator or other group members and gives her a sense of her own potency in being able to act effectively as an agent producing changes she decides to make in her own life.

Another tool used to promote problem-solving efficiency is *homework.* After a woman has a contract, she can be assigned or assign herself homework which she works on during the week. Homework is used to work on the long-range goal of the contract on a step-by-step basis. People are able to feel safe enough to make real changes in their lives by moving in stages and using a timing they feel they can handle rather than moving too fast in frightening leaps.

A blackboard can be used to diagram and explain the social transactions between people and is also used for women to "sign up" to work at the beginning of group. Signing up facilitates the work: it lets the members of the group know who wants to work, so that the entire group can take cooperative responsibility for everyone having enough time.

Another valuable tool has been Eric Berne's definitions of the three observable ego states. Berne proposed a system based on the observation that people act in three definitely different ways or modes, called *ego states*. They act like parents—people who *know* without questioning what's right and wrong and how things should be done. They act like adults—that is, they process information and make predictions from that data about the future like a computer without feelings. And they act like children—they can be creative, open, and direct; play; be in touch with exactly what they want and what their feelings are. Using these three ego states—*the Parent, the Adult,* and *the Child*—we can explain in group what's going on with people, help them demystify what's happening within themselves and what's happening in their transactions with others. For example, with the aid of ego states, it's possible to explain to a woman why she feels resentment when her husband repeatedly tells her how to do things. The transaction is supposedly Adult-Adult, but because of the repetition, she experiences it as his Parent giving orders to and dominating her Child (Figure 1). We in radical psychiatry feel that it is vital to be able to explain in easily understood language what goes on between people.

Our main goal in using language tools such as the ego states is to make it simple and easy for people to understand themselves and others in ways that have mystified them before.

It has been evident in women's groups that women have a lot of permission to use their Nurturing Parent;

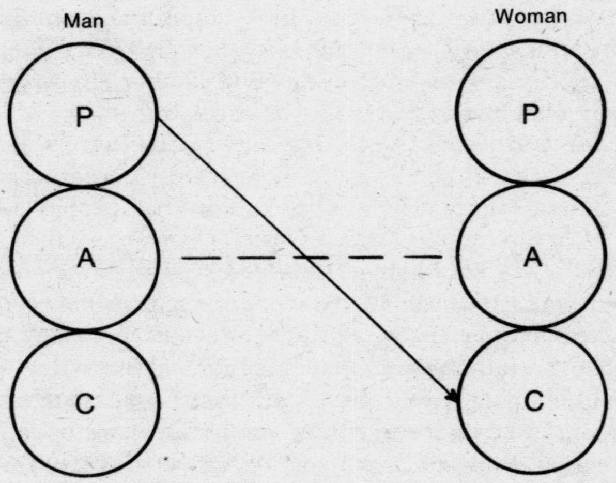

A Man Speaking to a Woman

that is, being loving and caring for other people. They also have permission to act in their Child, to be dependent, playful, intuitive, and needy. But it has also become obvious that women have little permission to use their Adult; that is, to be able to figure things out logically, to be intellectually potent and "take care of business." Women are enjoined from their earliest days *not* to use these powers. They are pressured not to develop skills that give them control over their lives, their bodies, or the means of production in society. They are encouraged to take care of and service the needs of others. They are taught to be good cooks or good housekeepers or good secretaries, but definitely not to know how to fix the car or how to figure things out. One of the main efforts we make in women's groups is to give women permission to use their Adult, to develop their rational power to get what their Child wants in life. Unfortunately, while women have a lot of permission to be nurturing to others, they have very little permission to love and take care of themselves *first.* Often in group it's necessary to teach women to love themselves, be their own best friend, and stop giving away *all* their loving and caring.

POLITICS OF THE PROBLEM-SOLVING GROUP

In radical psychiatry we approach problems from a radical political perspective. From this perspective we make certain assumptions about human beings. We assume that people are O.K.; that they are basically good and in their inner core wish to and are capable of living in peace and harmony with themselves, with each other, and with the earth. We believe that alienation is the result of mystified oppression: i.e., Alienation = Oppression + Mystification.

By *alienation* we mean a sense of not being right with

the rest of the world or humankind, a feeling of being not O.K. because something is wrong with you that makes you incapable of being happy and in tune with your world. The alienation that most women experience daily is enormous. It is shocking, for instance, to consider how many women are alienated from their own sexuality. Sound data isn't readily available, but a survey in *Psychology Today* which reported on a very select, relatively enlightened, and sexually free audience related that 20% of the women in the group said that during intercourse they reached orgasm never or almost never, and an additional 10% only one-fourth of the time. That is, 30% of these women achieve orgasm every four times they make love at the most.

Women have the right to have orgasm at least as often as men, but this won't come about if shrinks continue to listen to sexist theories like Freud's which cast women's sexuality in a demeaning light with accusations of penis envy and inadequacy. A woman's alienation from her sexuality causes her to feel that she is not O.K. Usually, she assumes she is "frigid" when, in actuality, if the oppressiveness of her situation was made apparent to her, she would view herself compassionately as a victim of the prejudices concerning women's sexuality.

Another form of alienation can be found in older women who are slandered as being bitchy or menopausally depressed when, in actuality, they are reaping the full thrust of an oppressive role in life. Because they have not pursued careers or been "producers" within the system, they receive little in the way of recognition for Adult work. Due to ageist and media prejudices about sexual beauty they are no longer considered viable love objects. And as for their roles as homemakers and mothers, they receive scant thanks for spending their lives sacrificing and caring for their families. Yet, when they become depressed about this unjust payoff, they often receive the outrageous punishment of electric shock therapy and/or stupefying drugs.

Further examples of alienation in women are: those who never decide to love themselves but are full of self-hate and contempt for themselves and other women; and women who see themselves as ugly and torture their minds and bodies, eternally vacillating between over-eating and disgust with their overweight bodies and going on torturous and ineffective diets, all the while mistaking their physical selves for their enemy.

The other vital element in this equation is the idea of *mystification,* which simply means deception. Women are deceived into colluding with their oppression; they are deceived into believing there is something wrong with them rather than understanding that they are being exploited, as in the case of the woman who considers herself frigid. Once mystification is removed, a woman can realize that she actually is being oppressed, and she will then no longer feel that *she* is not O.K. Once she can clearly see and taste this injury she can become angry and finally begin to move against the real culprit. We believe that Oppression + Awareness = Anger. The anger that comes from awareness is very useful to motivate women to use their Adult and focus their energy on fighting for and reclaiming their power.

The antithesis to Alienation or Mystified Oppression is Liberation—that is, Awareness + Contact = Action → Liberation. By *awareness* we mean the opposite of deception: consciousness. Consciousness must incorporate an understanding of the necessity for action. To be able to make your life better, you must seize control over it; thus you must *act.* Consciousness alone is not enough. Thought, when it excludes the necessity for action, is alienated. For thought not to become an alienated and disconnected headtrip, it must be grounded in practice; that is, based on real life experience. A psychiatric example of a headtrip without necessary action would be psychoanalysis, in which most people experience themselves as growing in understanding about themselves through dream analysis, etc., but still are not able to understand how to make real changes in their behavior.

We also believe that to overcome our oppression and gain liberation we need support and impetus from others. This is called contact. Women working in group need strokes and support from other women. Strokes are positive human recognition, examples of which would be a warm smile, a sincere compliment, a hug, a caress, or credit for hard work.

HOW RESCUE OPPRESSES WOMEN

We feel that it is vital that members of groups understand the sources of their oppression. We constantly work on awareness of how sex roles and capitalist society oppress people. But the idea we view as crucial is that, for people to feel better, for people to get what they want and "take care of business," they must act, they must move. People have to act to get what they want; they have to work for themselves in group and between meetings. To facilitate this work, women make a contract with the group to accomplish some definite goal. An example would be: "I want to ask for and accept strokes." No one can do this work for her; we can only help her work on it, and protect her when she gets scared. The ultimate responsibility for the decision to do it and the actual work to get there, lies with her.

We can't *Rescue* people who are oppressed. Rescue in this case means something very particular. It is an attempt to save someone whom you view and who views herself as helpless and powerless. To Rescue someone is oppressive and presumptuous, since it colludes with people's apathy and sense of impotence. Rather than demanding that people take power and ask for what they want, it reinforces people's passivity. The image it evokes is a world full of helpless consumers, powerless victims aching for visitation from powerful rescuers.

When two people play this game, they each take on one of three roles which they then constantly change. The three roles are Victim, Rescuer, and Persecutor (Figure 2), and are capitalized here to distinguish them from the true states of being a victim, rescuer, or persecutor.[2]

Here's an example from group:

Frances felt very sorry for her roommate, Sarah, whose lover was killed in an accident. She had a lot of sympathy for her and wanted very much to console her. But Sarah never seemed to feel better. For months she continued to feel bad and constantly wanted to tell Frances how hard it was not to have a man. After a while, Frances began to dread talking to Sarah, but she would listen (play the Rescuer role) because she felt guilty since her own relationships with her lovers were fine.

Frances couldn't see her way clear to tell her friend Sarah she didn't want to hear her complaints anymore. Finally, Frances began to get angry and think about moving out. She felt her friend was persecuting *her* because Sarah didn't work to make things better for herself. The group advised Frances to stop being angry (get out of the Persecutor role) and get into her Adult and have her Nurturing Parent available for her friend. The group told Frances to talk straight to Sarah, tell her how she felt about her playing the Victim role, and let her know she wanted her to start taking care of herself. As it turned out, it was hard for Sarah to take this feedback from Frances, but after she began working on it, she felt a lot better and let Frances know how much

---

[2] See Steven Karpman, "Script Drama Analysis," *Transactional Analysis Bulletin,* 7, 26 (1968).

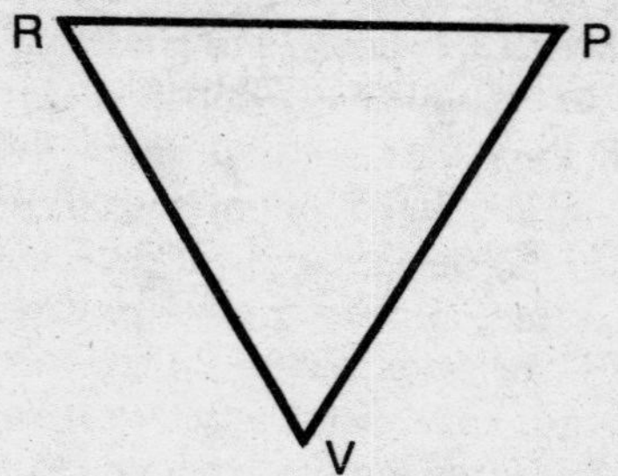

Drama Triangle

she appreciated her stopping the Rescue that might have destroyed their friendship and prolonged Sarah's period of mourning and self-pity.

I think in political terms we do people a great disservice when we attempt to Rescue them or to provide them with a consumable, feel-better therapy. We can help people by showing them new options they had been previously blinded to and teaching them problem-solving skills, but it's up to them to make the leap of faith to work through their fears about changing and taking power over their own lives. It's also up to them to do the struggling to learn to work cooperatively together in a group so that everyone can get what they want.

WOMEN'S OPPRESSION

There appear to be at least three realms in which women are oppressed. Women are oppressed in relation to themselves, that is, "within their own heads." They are oppressed in their intimate relationships with other individuals; and, finally, they are oppressed as members of society. In women's groups women can become familiar with what insidiously keeps them down—not only the obvious, overt male supremacy of which many of us are already aware and struggling against, but also oppression which has been internalized, which turns women against themselves, causing them to be their own worst enemy rather than their own loving best friend. This internalized oppression I have called the Pig Parent. It is the incorporation of all the values which keep women subordinate—messages saying, for example, that she mustn't outdo a man, she must be humble (i.e. not love herself), she must take care of others first, she must not be angry or bitchy; messages which also terrorize the Child part in her when it tries to be fine.

We see people acting in three different ways when they are behaving in their Child. They act as the *Natural Child,* that is, like a free child that is in touch with its feelings, acts spontaneously in behalf of them, and is creative and knows what it wants. They act as child-like Adults or like *Little Professors* whose intellect is intuitive rather than rational and logical. They act as the *Pig Parent,* which is the Parent in the Child. This is an immature, Child-like parent whose nurturing is conditional and not reliable. The Pig Parent only loves and cares for the Child as long as the Child adapts to what it wants. If the Child doesn't adapt, the Pig Parent withdraws its protection and support (Figure 3).

Women are oppressed in *all* their ego states. As I mentioned earlier, they are oppressed in their Nurturing Parent because in their roles as women they are enjoined to give all their nurturing away, to Rescue others, especially their husbands and children, but not to nurture themselves. In fact, if a woman is a loving, nurturing parent to herself she's seen as selfish, cold, and uncaring because she won't be self-sacrificing. Our goal in women's groups is to stop this absurd altruism and have all women love themselves *first.*

Women's groups are an excellent place for women to

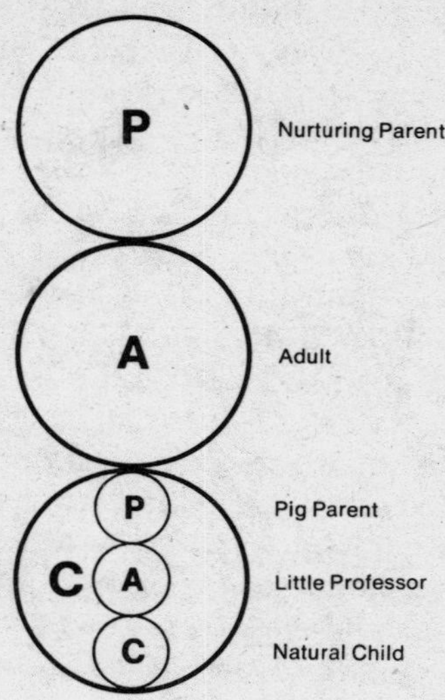

Ego States

feel safe enough to begin to use their Adult in a powerful way. They get support to use their intelligence, to think about things they have never thought about before, and to take the power to make decisions based on knowledge they hadn't previously given themselves credit for having. They are given an opportunity to experience and respect the intelligence of other women.

Women are made to feel crazy when men refuse to validate the intuitive perceptions of their Little Professor. Because men are often tuned out in this ego state, they often discount—that is, they refuse to account for many of the things women pick up on or are aware of intuitively. For instance, a woman who senses that her husband is loving her less and less each day is often discounted by him because when she asks him if he loves her he feels so guilty and scared that he has to lie to himself and her about his true feelings. Women also discount their own intuitive feelings and the feelings of others in the service of Rescuing them from the truth. They're afraid they'll have to deal with someone's anger or dislike of them.

Women are oppressed in their Natural Child; they don't feel safe enough in the world to do whatever they feel like doing. They tend to be what Maslow called "other directed"; that is, they look to others to see if it's O.K. to do certain things rather than just trusting their guts and doing what feels good.

When women nurture themselves, use their intelligence, trust their intuitions, and don't listen to their Pig Parent, they can act purely in behalf of what their Natural Child wants, which is their core—their center. We women can be truly powerful when we are in touch with this part of ourselves. Then can we know the truth of what feels right and what doesn't, what hurts and oppresses us, what causes us joy, fulfillment, or righteous anger.

The Nurturing Parent, Adult, Professor, and Natural Child are oppressed from the outside as well as within the Person. The Pig Parent is the enforcer of internal oppression.

The oppression by the Pig Parent can be easily illustrated by using a technique we call *bragging*. Children who feel O.K. about themselves love to tell how fine and wonderful they are until their parents and other grown-ups teach them that it is really bad (conceited, narcissistic) to truly like yourself and even worse to tell other people about it. Children believe this lie and often grow up unable to really love themselves. It is regretfully easy for a person to get in touch with their Pig. They merely need to get up in front of friends and tell them what they like about themselves, especially forbidden subjects, such as that they take delight in their body, or the way they look, or the way they make love. They will often experience anxiety and begin to qualify what they want to say. The Pig in their head wants them to be humble, and its messages are like these: "You'll make a fool of yourself because nobody believes that about you" or "Shut up, you're boring them."

When women are acting in their Pig Parent ego state they are constantly comparing and measuring their performance and productiveness. Their attitude toward themselves is demanding, not accepting. Things are never good enough. This internalized form of oppression can be devastating. In women's groups we are very interested in helping women "off" (destroy) their Pigs. In group it is important for women to become aware of the Pig and its messages as a powerful element of their oppression. To overcome it, women should be sensitized to when it makes them feel bad or actually says negative things about them. It's helpful to anticipate when the Pig may become active. It usually comes down heaviest when the Child wants to be out doing what she really wants (ignoring the dictates of the Pig), or when she has been feeling fine. It is often helpful to get in touch with what the Pig says and become familiar with its language. It often uses words like "must, should, ought, better, best, bad, stupid, ugly, crazy, or sick." Pigs also have *programs* which are ways of operating and carrying out its plans. It's important to figure the Pig's program. An example of a Pig program might be for someone to be so scared all the time that she can't get in touch with her real feelings and what she really wants in life. The way in which the Pig Parent would enforce this program would be by making threats to the person about frightening things that were supposedly going to happen. Pig messages are literally heard as voices speaking within the head, like a repetitive tape recording.

Sometimes Pig Programs operate like a vicious circle; certain patterns of behavior or thoughts get set up that are difficult to escape once the cycle begins. An example of this might be a woman who never asks for what she wants. She only asks for what she thinks people have for her. She wants to avoid putting anyone on the spot or being turned down. In other words, she Rescues people from how she actually feels and what she actually wants. When she does finally ask for something, she *really* wants it. So she applies a lot of pressure to get it. If she doesn't get it, she feels very bad and ripped off. Her Pig then gets a victory, because it can then say, "See, it doesn't pay to ask for what you want!" So then she asks even less for what she wants and feels even worse when she doesn't get it. The only way out of this cycle is for her to make a decision that radically changes her behavior—to ask for 100% of what she wants 100% of the time. She thus stops Rescuing people from her desires, and lets them take care of themselves by accepting a "no" answer from them without playing on their guilt by being a Victim. Because she'll be getting a lot more of what she wants, she won't be so disappointed about things she doesn't get; and, overall, she'll be having more of what she wants when she wants it.

To be sure, some people will sometimes do things for her which they don't want to do; that is, they'll Rescue her. And since Rescuers inevitably become Persecutors, she will have to absorb some anger from some people. But the benefits of asking for what she wants far outweigh the problems that accompany it, since they defeat the Pig Parent that says: "You don't deserve anything; there is no use in asking." She also can let them know she resents their Rescue and not relate to people who won't stop doing it.

OFFING THE PIG PARENT

It is vital to work out good, solid responses to the Pig Parent when offing the oppression within and replacing it with a humane and tolerant view of oneself. This tolerant view is the Nurturing Parent's. It is important to create a Nurturing Parent for oneself which is free of contaminated statements. That is, to be sure that the nurturing is complete and straight, not an inverted Pig message saying "You're not ugly" rather than something completely positive like "You are beautiful." Along with making a decision not to listen to or empower their Pig Parent, it is vital that women decide to become their own best friend and stop working against themselves. I want to emphasize that most women must strengthen their Adult since it is crucial for making decisions. The ability to think rationally and make decisions is necessary to attain a solid sense of identity as an effective human being.

Two valuable inter-related techniques developed by Steiner[3] are *Permission* and *Protection*.

Permission is given to the Child to do things she wants to do, but which the Pig won't allow. Following the giving of permission, the leader and other group members must provide protection in the form of strokes and support. The facilitator must be potent when giving permission that goes against the original parental injunctions. She must be strong and sure of what she says and back up her permission with protection by being available together with the group to give support with her presence in group or over the telephone. In giving permission and protection she uses her own Nurturing Parent ego state to reassure the person against the Pig, whereas ordinarily she uses her Adult in most of the group interactions.

The notion of permission and protection is vital also in helping women to stop following *banal scripts*.[4]

---

[3] Claude Steiner, *Games Alcoholics Play: The Analysis of Life Scripts* (New York: Grove Press, 1971).

[4] *Ibid.* See also: Claude Steiner, *Scripts People Live* (New York: Grove Press, 1974).

Banal scripts are life styles or ways of being that are chosen early in life, decisions to live one's life by a certain plan that fits in with the Pig's program.

Women are enjoined to live their lives following sex-role scripts. Commonly, at an early age, a woman is given a doll and a dollhouse and told she should be a good mommy and housekeeper. Such messages are incorporated, and women are often acting in behalf of these sorts of parental messages rather than living their lives autonomously and for themselves, guided by their own true desires. In group we give women permission to get in touch with what they really want and then to go after it and get it.

THE GROUP IN ACTION

It's crucial that women be turned on to what's good about changing. They have to be able to taste what's yummy about it; what's in it for them. To get people to take risks it's often necessary to entice them, seduce them to make the leap of faith that is going to get them there. This often happens through testimonials by group members who have already done this, by exciting Child descriptions in group of what the payoff is like, and also by object lessons. For example, a woman who has a contract to ask for what she wants will be much more motivated if she practices it in group and gets an opportunity to enjoy the reward for her efforts in that safe situation.

I'd like to give some sense of how a successful group feels in action. A good group might look as follows: Attendance is high and prompt. Members who are interested in working sign up. Anyone in crisis puts a circle around her name.

An example of a group interaction might be: Jane wants to work. Her contract has been established as "I want to be able to know what I want, and be myself with others." She wants to work on this contract because all her life she has adapted to other people. She acts on the basis of what others want her to be, rather than on her own standards and desires. Today she reports that she's having trouble at work. She feels that she's lost touch with her co-workers. Her job is very oppressive and working conditions are dehumanizing. The group sympathizes with her oppression and advises her not to take action alone, but to try to organize her co-workers so that they can all make demands and get satisfaction as a group. Jane works hard giving and getting feedback from the group on this problem. She talks about how to take power in this situation, and the group gives her strokes for her hard work. She asks for homework, and the group recommends that she work at talking straight to people at work and getting their support to take care of business there. This woman is well-liked. The members of the group care deeply about her, and she gets the strokes that she wants. Jane has worked well in group and done much to transform herself and her life. She has struggled against things that were inhibiting her and done much to make her political awareness a part of her everyday personal life.

A recurrent discussion in women's groups is the issue of women Rescuing their children. In the stereotypic program of the nuclear family it's Mom's job to take care of everyone. The assumption is that she's supposed to do things for her kids for gratis. In return, they should obey her, love her, etc. This sets up a Rescue triangle. Mom is the Rescuer doing good things for the kids. They are helpless Victims who supposedly can't take care of themselves. (It's my paranoid belief that this is a conspiracy to teach children that they are powerless in the world.) Thus her children are kept dependent and basically experience themselves as not having power. But as they fail to do what they are told to do, Mom eventually feels unloved and Victimized by them because she's already over-extended and she comes to view them as Persecuting her.

Once she's accumulated enough held resentments, she can cash them in by "pigging" the children. She then becomes the Persecutor to their Victim until she feels guilty. And once again the roles switch—and on and on it goes. The only way out is for her to completely reappraise her living situation in her Adult. She has to decide to give up the fairy tale of the happy nuclear family and decide to begin living collectively; that is, act as if she were living in a commune, where everyone is expected to work cooperatively and take responsibility for making the collective work by contributing all they can to the situation. This gives children an opportunity to use their power, to ask for what they want, and for parents to give only what they want to give and to also get things back from their children.

Here's an example of how this problem was worked on in group by one woman who has two adolescent children. Her contract is: "I want to know what I want and get it." She complained to the group that after working her boring and badly paid job all week, she has to spend all day Saturday cleaning her house, with little or no help from her kids or the man she lives with. Because she feels bad she Persecutes everybody on Saturday and by Sunday everyone's feeling bad and her weekend is shot. The group gave her feedback about how she plays Rescue and gave her homework to take care of herself and ask her family clearly and strongly for what she wants. They pointed out to her that her family may not understand what she wants from them or what's in it for them if they cooperate. The group's feedback sunk in, and soon she announced to the group that things were much better. During the week she had come home from work and found a sink full of dishes. She refused to cook dinner until the dishes were done and sat in the living room just taking care of herself. This sit-down strike was a really good object lesson for her lover and children. They let her know the next day that they wanted to have a house meeting and figure out how to work together better.

The women in the group were really pleased she had taken care of herself and gave her lots of strokes. The following week she told us that, working together, they had gotten the house clean Saturday morning and had the afternoon open to go play and enjoy each other for a change.

The following is an example of a history of a woman who has been in group for a little over a year. When she came into group she was frightened and felt helpless about being able to take care of herself and get what she wanted in life. She was constantly playing the role of a Victim and looking for a Rescuer. She would engage in playing "Ain't it Awful?" (which is a futile game of complaining about oppression but not working to change anything and which co-opts a person's energy and keeps her passive). She would describe how much of a Victim she was; and when group members would make suggestions about what she could do about it, she would make excuses and play "Yes, But. . . ." A year ago she had been "diagnosed" at a clinic as "agitated depression." Her general stance in group was that she wanted other people to do something for her and take care of her rather than to do something for herself and take responsibility over her own life.

I'd like to describe briefly the dialectical process of this woman's contracts with the group; that is, the different stages by which her work in group proceeded.

First, she started with a contract to get her Pig off her back. This contract was vague and served only to help us get a sense of what her Pig Program was. This evolved into a contract to talk straight. For the first time in her life she told people how she really felt about them and began getting in touch with her true feelings. The contract changed then into being able to say what she thought or felt at a given time. This helped her to be spontaneously in touch with herself. Her final contract is to be powerful for herself. In the first six months of her work in group this woman would repeatedly make phone calls to me which she attempted to stretch to twenty or thirty minutes. She would be very frightened and looking for a Rescue and showed little interest in taking care of business for herself. With the awareness that she has gotten in group, plus support from group members, she has slowly learned to take care of herself and assume responsibility for her own life. Now, if she calls, she asks for something specific which can usually be given in five minutes, like: information, reassurance, or strokes. She no longer looks for people to Rescue her and resents it when people do. She is interested in getting support from others and information as to what she can do to take care of things for herself. She comes to group and works hard and prefers to assign herself homework rather than having it assigned to her.

I believe that she will soon be leaving group; and, as has been the case with other women, she will then have completed her contract and have a sense of closure. She will feel that she has gotten what she wanted and will take away with her skills and ability to solve her own and others' problems and be able to take power over her own life. It will also be evident to her that she cannot get everything she wants in life on her own as an individual, that solutions will have to come through working with others. She knows if she gets in trouble in her head she can ask some friend who has been in group and knows how to problem-solve to get together with her and help her. If she gets into hassles with another person she can ask a friend to meet with her and the other person to mediate their difficulties.

She understands that the game of Rescue is vicious

and debilitating, and it robs people of their power. It keeps them from talking straight to each other and having the power to get what they want. She is now keenly aware that there are definite forces in society that keep her from having a full and happy life, that there are power structures invested in robbing her of her full humanity. For example, she is clearly aware of sexism and how it affects her possibilities of getting needed strokes.

RELATING TO MEN

A constant source of problems for women in group are their loving relationships with men. The Pig Program seems to be for women to fall in love with men, not get what they want, and then be very hurt and go into a "depression." Women consistently refuse to use their Adults in their loving relationships; they follow their Child feelings and are rudely surprised and hurt when they come up against the reality of where the men they are relating to are really at. When relationships fail, women think there's something wrong with *them*. But, for the most part, the trouble lies in the fact that men and women have very different attitudes about how to be in life. Often, men are not as interested in struggling as women are. They're either happy where they are at, or are too scared to change; or, due to the comfort of their privileged position, they are changing very slowly. Women in group, on the other hand, are for the most part eager to change. But their old scripting about loving relationships sets them up to be hurt. They are so desirous of being loved and finding someone to love that they often fall in love with their own Child fantasies rather than the actual person. They seem to be out of control, and they experience their loving feelings as dominating them: "I can't help myself. I know he doesn't love me the way I love him, but I can't stop feeling the way I do." Their feelings have *them* rather than *they* having their feelings.

The way out of this powerlessness and exploitation is for women to take a long, hard look, with their Adults, at the men whom they have empowered. They need to decide not to love anyone who doesn't love them back, and keep their loving feelings equal with those of whomever they're relating to, and decide *first* to be in love with themselves, and then exchange love with others.

Many women who feel disappointed in their relationships with men have decided to give up struggling with them completely. They've found they can get a lot more satisfaction and appreciation in loving relationships with other women. They can develop strong friendships and enjoy the richness of other women's nurturing, intuition, intelligence, strength, and sexuality.

GROUP COLLUSIONS

One of the pitfalls of women's groups is that there may develop group collusions. There might be subtle agreements between group members not to talk straight about certain things, or not to press each other about certain problems. This *keeping of secrets* can become part of the group culture, its "Karma." An example of this might be a group that encourages its members to look for a Rescue. Women are pressed to feel like Victims, to be powerless, to feel sorry for themselves and each other; but they have little permission to be Adults, to talk straight, to be potent, to take their power and take care of business, and to get what they want. Women in group may make a covert deal to give each other strokes and protection in order not to have to talk straight. In a group like this the facilitator can demystify what her Professor is sensing and what she sees going on. The facilitator can ask that people talk about solutions and what can be done about problems, rather than have them talk in detail about how bad things are or how heavy the problem is. She also should give people strokes for working and not going with their Pig and encourage others to give strokes for being powerful and taking care of business.

A useful tool for demystifying what's going on in a group is the process of letting go of *held resentments*, or "stamps."[5] The process, as worked out in radical psychiatry, is done in the following manner.

It may be decided, usually at the beginning of a group, to "do stamps." People will say to each other, "I have a stamp for you, do you want it?" The other person says "yes" or "no" depending on whether or not she feels strong enough to accept critical feedback. It is understood that a stamp may be quite paranoid, that it can be "off the wall," and that it is often generated by a misunderstanding; that is why no discussion or disagreement is allowed to follow stamp-giving. This is how it's done: "I was angry at you when you didn't talk to me at the party on Saturday." The person receiving this may say nothing, or "I hear you," and it is let go at that. The resentment is given some time to sink in; and if further discussion is needed, it can be taken care of at a later time. No one is given more than one in a row.

At the same time that held resentments are let go, so are *paranoid fantasies*. An example might be: "I think you've got a secret you're not telling the group." The person given the paranoid fantasy will then answer; and often there is at least a grain of truth in the paranoia.

I want to make it clear that people are urged to talk straight in the here and now and encouraged not to hold resentments or paranoid fantasies. But people don't

---

[5] See "Trading Stamps" in Eric Berne's *Principles of Group Treatment* (New York: Oxford University Press, 1966).

always do that, so this is an efficient way to keep things clean between people in groups.

After all the stamps and paranoias have been given out, people then give strokes; often, when people are holding stamps, they are also holding strokes they haven't felt free to give. Stamps, paranoias, and strokes are powerful antidotes against collusions in groups.

CONCLUSION

I think one of the most important aspects of group work is to stress teaching people to work cooperatively together. All of our Pig programming teaches us to compete and consume each other, not cooperate and create each other. In group, women can cooperate on making sure they share the time, work hard on each other's contracts, talk straight, keep no secrets, and not Rescue each other.

One of the most important jobs of a facilitator is to teach people to take back their power. While turning people on to new options in life and skills in problem-solving, it is necessary that she demand that people take as much responsibility as they can for what happens in group. The goal isn't to build dependency relationships or admiration for the facilitator, but rather to work on a constant transferral of power and expertise. I encourage women to challenge my work in group. I welcome criticism and feedback and work hard to respond to it. I don't work on my own problems in group, but I do mention relevant experiences I've had, so women know I'm fighting the same oppression that they are coming up against. I answer any questions they have about my own life and strive to be absolutely transparent in group about how I feel while I'm there. I work in my Adult to give information, with my Nurturing Parent available to give support and strokes, and with my Child ready for a good laugh or joyous smile at someone's latest victory.

In closing, I want to stress that we in radical psychiatry begin with a definite radical political perspective. We are not interested in being "hip" shrinks who service counter-culture people. We are community organizers; we want to teach people problem-solving skills, political awareness; and we want to provide protection to people while they make changes they want to make in their lives. But the ultimate responsibility for this happening rests equally in the hands of the group members—not just with the facilitators. We desire to put people in touch with their power. Our aim is to impart problem-solving skills and teach people to take power over their own lives. We are interested in having people reclaim themselves as full and potent human beings. We believe that the group situation is the most auspicious for women, since the group process obviously indicates that there are no individual solutions for oppressed people and that to have strength we must band together.

It is especially valuable for women to interact with other women and develop a keen sense of sisterhood. The group structure is also very efficient for problem-solving work since it provides much diversified feedback. Still, I also feel it is important to make clear here that complete human liberation is not possible in our present capitalist society. Individuals cannot be free from sex-role oppression in a society where such oppression is built-in as an integral part of how the economy maintains itself. For individuals to be free, society must be free. Women cannot overcome social oppression as individuals. Only by working cooperatively together can we become powerful enough to make the substantive changes that we want in our world.

8. PERMISSION by Hogie Wyckoff

Permission work acts is complimentary to work done in a problem-solving group. It provides the necessary time, room, and equipment that is not available in a regular radical psychiatry group. Permission is done when specifically needed, whereas problem-solving is ongoing.

Permission exercises are designed to help people do things they want to do, but can't, because they have internalized prohibitive and inhibitive parental messages. For example, a person's real desire and need may be to be able to ask for the strokes (a hug, a kiss, etc.) she or he wants, but their Pig Parent says, "NO! Don't you dare!"

A useful means for understanding people (which I shall explain here because it is integral to understanding permission) is to observe that they behave in three distinctive modes, or ego states: the *Parent, Adult,* and *Child.* In the Parent ego state the person may be Nurturing or Critical. The Nurturing Parent is the part of them that is unconditionally loving and accepting. The Pig Parent is critical and unaccepting, always demanding a performance, perfection, and saying: "Not good enough." The Child is the part of a person that plays, is creative and free, and does what it likes to do.

In order to help a person be able to ask for strokes, the person leading the exercise must provide *three P's:* Permission, Protection, and Potency.[1] Permission is approval given to the Child to do what she wants. Protection is safety provided by the leader's Nurturing Parent. It is absolutely necessary that the person leading the exercise be nurturing to the people doing it. Potency is the strength to back up what you say, carry through on it, and deal head-on with someone else's Pig Parent. In the above example I would say: "Okay, I want you to ask someone here for a stroke." I would *insist* that the person did this (assuming we had a *contract* between us specifying what she wanted to work on). If she got frightened, I would reassure her; if someone else pigged her, I would protect her; and if her own Pig came in on her, I'd help her get rid of it. I wouldn't back down or "chicken out"; yet I would be very sensitive to where the person was at and be as supportive and responsive to her individual needs as I could while teaching her a new way to be.

As I said, it is necessary to have an agreement, a contract arrived at ahead of time in their problem-solving group (Chapter 6). The contract should state simply and clearly what the Child wants. It is necessary that the contract be capable of being fulfilled here and now in the permission class situation. Thus a contract for a woman to have orgasm during intercourse is not valid for permission class because this couldn't be accomplished in that setting. It is very helpful to write the contracts up on a wall with large crayons where everyone can see them. It should be understood that no one has to do anything that they don't want to do. People who change their minds are free to terminate the contract.

Permission exercises are not a pacification of people's

[1] Claude Steiner, *Scripts People Live* (New York: Grove Press, 1974).

alienation as many touchy–feely–good–vibe therapy techniques are. This is because Permission in radical psychiatry is not just giving people contact but involves awareness as well; therefore, we talk about what happens and provide the necessary consciousness raising for true liberation. We don't want to co-opt the potential of people to discover for themselves how they are oppressed and to become angry enough to do something about it. We don't have angry women just beat on pillows so as to pacify themselves temporarily. We help them learn new ways of being and help them learn how to get what they want. So, in keeping with our example, I would explain how the stroke economy (see Chapter 3) exploits us in our lovings, and not just do a magic trick for someone.

It is important to ask people how they are feeling when doing exercises. Keep communication open. Let people talk about their experiences and get and give feedback.

In doing permission exercises, no one is giving anyone anything they didn't originally have. People are born O.K., but oppressed away from their full human potential.

It is often very useful, although not necessary, to use appropriate music when doing different exercises. This helps bring out the Free Child and set the mood. Throughout this chapter I will give examples of various types of applicable music.

When starting a class I tell people that this is a safe situation—and I mean it. They can do whatever they want to do except hit each other without fear of implied promises, especially sexual, to others in what they do. This allows people to be spontaneous and free without the usual social prohibitions and fears of unwanted commitments.

There are generally five types of exercises, and I will present them in the order in which they should be used:

Introduction and Trust; Stroking; Getting O.K.; Being O.K.; and *Fantasy.* I also will give examples of each and explain how they are done.

Four aspects of each exercise will be discussed. First, how the exercise is being done and how contact between people is made. Second, what the purpose of the exercise is and what it means. Third, how the exercise looks when it is done correctly and provides a liberating experience. Fourth, how in some cases the exercise can go wrong and make people feel even more alienated.

Some exercises marked with an asterisk I will only refer to briefly.

I. INTRODUCTION AND TRUST

Say Your Name

Standing in a large circle, have people say their name to the rest of the group. Tell them to say it loud and clear; let it resonate. Have them walk into the center of the circle when they say it and/or have them say it three times, in different ways.

The purpose is for people to present themselves to others and to make a first step in learning to "brag" (more on this later); that is, to be able to say good things about themselves.

People should make their names heard and give each name time to "soak in." It should be similar to a mini show-and-tell about the person doing it.

Introduce Each Other

Have people choose a partner and find out their name and the most important things about them. Then have the partners take turns introducing and telling about each other to the rest of the group.

The purpose is to have people quickly and intuitively learn about each other. Also, to drop trivial conversation and really find out about other people; that is, make intimate contact.

People should be able to discover what's important about each other in human terms. If there are too many people, it's O.K. to limit what they say to two or three things they were told and something they saw but were not told. The introductions should be honest and some feeling of intimacy achieved.

Large Trust Circle

Have everyone take off their shoes and stand in a circle. (You need at least eight to ten people to do this.) Each person will then take a turn going into the center of the circle, closing their eyes, turning around to disorient themselves, then walking as fast as they feel it is safe to do, moving out to the edge of the circle. They should keep their hands at their sides, have their chins out, and walk straight on, not sideways or with their heads down. People at the edge will catch them with their hands, which are held out ready, while they are well balanced with their feet braced securely. The "catchers" will lean forward slightly to avoid stubbed toes, catch the person, and gently turn her around, pointing her in a new direction. If the person gets frightened, be nurturing with them.

Be sure that the situation *is* really safe. Make sure people can't trip on a rug or hurt themselves.

The purpose of this is for people to learn they can count on others in the group. Also, it's a good chance to practice being trustworthy and a Nurturing Parent to others when they are frightened and need reassurance.

The leader must be tuned in to the person working. Keep in close communication with her; find out what she is feeling and help her feel safe enough to trust.

This may involve telling people to go slower when they are pushing themselves to go faster than feels safe to them, or telling them to take a peek when it's obvious they're having a hard time keeping their eyes shut, or, if they get really scared, taking their hand and walking with them until they feel safe. People will usually start out slowly and a little afraid and build trust and then be able to take chances. They may even be able to run or at least really get off-balance and trust the group. People who are the most afraid will often be the last to try it. Let them do what feels good. This is not a performance. People should learn something, not get their minds blown. People should eventually look comfortable while doing this exercise.

It's important that people don't pull tricks on each other, such as backing off and making the circle larger that it was to begin with. It's also not good for the "catchers" to push the other person off in another direction; they should only be pointed.

People who are afraid may have a counter-phobic response and just jump in, as into a cold pool of water. Don't let them frighten their Child too badly by staying out of touch with their fear and by pushing themselves.

If someone is very afraid, they shouldn't do it; perhaps they should try a Small Trust Circle (see later exercise).

Blind Walk*

Have people choose partners and take turns leading each other around on a walk with eyes closed. It's best if done outside and people turn each other on to things that smell and feel good like flowers, people's hair and skin, etc.

People learn to trust and be nurturing to each other.

People should take good care of each other and have fun and get in touch with their senses. When feeling really trusting, people can get into doing a blind run with their partner.

The Small Trust Circle

Have about eight people stand in a tight, close circle and gently pass back and forth a person standing in the center who should stand straight, knees stiff, feet together, eyes closed, and body relaxed.

People learn to trust the whole group in close contact. It's easier than the Large Trust Circle for some people.

It works if the person relaxes and relinquishes control. The head should hang and the body should be off-balance.

II. STROKES

Group Massage

Have a person needing strokes lie down on their stomach or back as they choose on a mat. Have the group kneel around the person and ask one of the group to lead the massage. This leader can tap, pat, slap, etc., while everyone else follows what she is doing. If a person is particularly needy of loving strokes, it is best to give them just that: loving, tender stroking. People who are scared of getting strokes are most able to accept being touched on their back. If the person receiving is rigid, unable to accept strokes, talk to them in a nurturing and reassuring way and ask them to relax.

The purpose is to give strokes to people who want them but have little permission either to accept them or ask for them. It's a good way to give a lot of strokes to a needy person in a short amount of time.

The person being stroked should have her eyes closed and let the strokes "soak in." People giving strokes should not get into small talk with each other, but rather concentrate on giving. When it's over, time should be taken while the person gets up, opens her eyes, and *sees* everyone caring about her.

Music: anything quiet and soothing (not necessary).

Stroke Mill

Everyone closes their eyes and walks around the room touching other people. Have them explore each other's hands, hair, faces, etc. Guide the mill with instructions geared to the group's tolerance for accepting physical strokes.

The purpose is to let people touch and be touched freely in a safe situation without the usual emphasis on touching necessarily meaning a sexual advance.

People maintain awareness of their Child's innermost desires about what's happening and go with them either to touch or to move away from someone according to what feels good, without forcing themselves to do anything that feels unpleasant.

It is alienated when people adapt to what other people want, not staying in touch with and taking care of their own desires.

Music: "Spirit in the Dark"; "What the World Needs Now."

Trash the Stroke Economy*

After explaining the basic rules of the stroke economy (i.e., don't ask for strokes you want; don't give strokes you have; don't accept the strokes you get; don't reject strokes you don't want; and don't stroke yourself), have everyone stand in a circle, taking turns being in the center. Whoever is in the center does something to break down the imposed scarcity of strokes between people. They can ask for, receive, give, or reject strokes, or stroke themselves. An example would be to ask a particular person for a hug and to accept it if she gave it, or accept her declining the invitation if she refused, not as a put-down, but merely move on to ask someone else.

People can commit revolutionary actions in a limited way in this safe situation by breaking oppressive rules and seeing that it can feel good to do so when there is protection.

People undermine the usual shortage of strokes, and give and take strokes freely.

It is alienated if people adapt; that is, they give or accept strokes when they don't want to or when they adapt to other people's wants.

III. TO GET O.K.

Use the Nurturing Parent (in Three Steps)

STEP ONE: THE WORDS

Using your "other hand" (your left if you're right-handed, or vice versa), with large crayons on big sheets of paper write words or phrases on one side of the paper that describe what your Child would like its N.P. (Nurturing Parent) to be like. The words should be Child-type words, such as: "loves me," "is big and gentle," "holds me," etc.

On the other side of the paper, write what your Child would like your N.P. to say to you: "I love you"; "You're beautiful"; etc. Have everyone share the descriptions of their N.P. and after that read aloud the things they would like to hear from their N.P.

This is a good way for people to get in touch with the quality of their N.P. They can learn what other people's N.P.s are like and also not to be embarrassed to use nurturing, loving words. Let people take their words home with them to use on themselves whenever they need them.

When sharing their lists, people should say the words they want to hear, in the way they want to hear them (warmly, lovingly, etc.), and let them soak in. Everyone will feel warm and good when they are said. Some people may even get homesick and cry.

It is alienated when the words are said in the Adult, or, if the words are subtle reversals of Pig Parent words, such as: "You're not ugly." If this happens, the leader (or other people in the group) should intervene and help to elicit a straight N.P. stroke, like: "You're beautiful."

STEP TWO: SAY THE WORDS TO EACH OTHER

Have people give their words to someone they like; then have that person say the words to her partner while she holds that person on her lap or cuddles him in some way.

It gives people practice in being N.P. to others who need it, and to learn to accept the N.P. that they want from others. It also gets people in touch with their basic goodness and their caring for one another.

People should touch each other and not be afraid to be comforting. They should let the words soak in and not go too fast. People can ask to hear their words repeated as much as they want.

STEP THREE: NURTURING PARENT MILL

Have people close their eyes and mill around the room. When people come in contact with each other, have them be nurturing and loving to the Child in the other person, touching them in a nurturing way and saying N.P. words.

After being N.P. to each other, have them be N.P. to

themselves (e.g. give themselves a hug and say good things to themselves).

This teaches people to be nurturing to others and themselves and to be able to accept nurturing. It also helps break down the stroke economy between people and their own failure to stroke themselves. It gets in touch with the basic O.K.-ness of the group.

This is similar to the regular stroking mill. It works if people do only what feels good.

People should feel free to give and accept nurturing strokes. People should feel that they are really O.K.

It is alienated when people adapt; that is, go through the motions because they think they "should"—but they really don't want to. It's also alienated if it's done in the Adult, not in a warm, loving way.

Music: "Bridge Over Troubled Water"; "You've Got a Friend"; "Let It Be"; "Once There Was a Way."

Off the Pig

This is a powerful exercise requiring skill and great care. Expertise in working with people is definitely necessary to do it right. You must have a contract, an agreement with the person to "off their Pig." It should come after the N.P. exercise and in some ways is similar to it. Only two or three people should do it at any one period of time; the rest of the group (composed preferably of more people) should remain in their N.P. for support. It's a struggle to off the Pig Parent; and when a leader agrees to do it she has to be potent, aware of what's going on, and persistent enough to carry it through.

With the "other hand" and using crayons on large paper have people write on one side Child words or phrases to describe what their Pig is like: "mean, stupid, sneaky, etc."; and on the other side what the Pig tells them: "You're crazy, no one likes you, etc." On a smaller sheet have them draw a face mask depicting their Pig. Then they should read the descriptions and the words of their Pig aloud. Have people act out their Pig non-verbally, using their body and sounds, always with their mask held up to their face. Have them use the words their Pig uses on them. Have them give you their words (for your reference) while they work through destroying their Pig (in the form of the mask).

This teaches people how to get their Pig off their backs. They learn what it is like; what words it uses; how it acts; and the emotions it uses to oppress. People can learn a strategy for fighting their Pig by knowing how it functions as the enemy. This shows them that they can do it, and that other people will back them up. They should get encouragement from others while they're doing it. They thus learn how to answer it, how to stop it, and a means of neutralizing it in the future.

To be effective in this exercise, the person must combine into one forceful act three all-important elements: the right *words, emotion,* and *action.* All three must be present at the same time; otherwise, the Pig won't leave. Without all three present, it would be like trying to get rid of a tricky person just by being angry, or trying to get rid of a bully through words alone. You need a clever strategy to deal with a tricky person and some sort of force or anger to get rid of a bully. Trust your guts while leading this to know if the Pig has really been "offed." It should feel obvious and definite when it happens and end with a flourish of finality.

Others in the room can give all the nurturing needed by the other people to do something scary.

After people "off" their Pig, they should get all the strokes they want from whomever they want. A celebration usually happens because this exercise is scary and feels like a real victory when done well.

It won't work if people don't really want to do it. If someone realizes she doesn't want to go on, let her out of her contract. It's definitely not done right unless *all* three parts of the offing are there. The right emotion and action without the right words won't do it. People have to be able to answer their Pigs to shut them up. Words and emotion without action, or any other combination of merely two elements, will be ineffectual. The leader should allow no Pig Parent behavior during this exercise. Do not let anyone "pig" the person working to try to goad them into action or anger. People feel good after they successfully "off" the Pig, not sad or afraid or doubtful.

IV. I'M O.K.

Bragging

Have the person who wants to brag stand where everyone can see her and say all the good things she can think of to say about herself. Not just things she does, but also things she is. Have her say things she likes about her body and how she looks. Be sure to explain that it's not competitive, and therefore not proper to use comparisons like "better," etc.

This teaches people that although the word "bragging" has a bad connotation in our society it's not a bad thing to do so long as it's not competitive. It trashes the stroke economy and allows people to publicly dig on themselves and see that others like them when they do.

They should use positive words that describe themselves, not comparative words or inverted Pig messages, like "I look good for someone who is so fat." People should cheer each other on and generally be supportive to and appreciative of someone who brags.

It is alienated when people use sentences with negative or relative words, like "I'm not bad" or "I'm better than." It's alienated also if they only talk about *what* they do, not *who* they are; or if they qualify the good things they say about themselves; or if they don't say anything good about their physical selves.

Move to Music as Free Child*

Have everyone close their eyes and listen to music. Ask them to start moving slowly and let the music move them. Ask them not to do familiar dance patterns.

This helps people to move freely and to experience new motions in their bodies.

This should be free and open, with movements loose and spontaneous.

Music: "I Wish I Knew How It Would Feel To Be Free."

Be In the Center: Follow the Leader*

Have people take turns being in the center, moving to music while people follow them in a "follow the leader" game.

This shows people that it's O.K. to be in the center of attention, and frees people to lead.

Music: "Working Together."

V. FANTASY

Trips for Discovery

People can take fantasy trips for growth and discovery. Have people lie back, close their eyes, breathe deeply, and relax while you take them on a trip. An example would be: taking people on a long hike to the top of a mountain where they can ask a wise person only one question. What do they ask? Or: "You have died. It's your funeral. You're in the coffin. Who's there at your funeral? What do they say to you? What do you want to say to them? Say goodbye to people until there is only one person left. Who is it?" The leader should go slowly and permit fantasy to develop.

This helps get people in touch with things they may not be in touch with.

It's useful when people are relaxed and get into it. They should be able to talk about it later.

Music: Soft and airy mood music.

Role-Play Opposite Sex

Have people be the opposite sex. Men can pretend they're in short skirts and high heels while women can see themselves in men's trousers, etc. Have the "men" ask the "women" for a date, for strokes, etc.

A sex-role inversion can be very useful to highlight oppression and mystification. Role-playing is generally very enlightening.

It's right if people are sincere about learning about sex roles. It's O.K. to have fun doing this exercise.

Section IV
Community Organizing

9. RADICAL PSYCHIATRY AND COMMUNITY ORGANIZING by Joy Marcus, Peter LaRiviere, and Daniel Goldstine

INTRODUCTION (by Joy Marcus)

Our emotional life is entwined with our political life. The muscle and blood of political life is the distribution of power. As long as there exists in our society an inequitable distribution of power based on economic wealth in tandem with racial, sexual, and class prejudices no one (no one I know, anyway) will be able to fully realize their human possibilities. But it also seems true that a healthy society would be made up of healthy people. For these reasons we are concerned with the problem of simultaneously changing how we are as individual organisms and radically changing society.

During a class session in radical psychiatry given at the Free University in Berkeley, we talked about doing a form of community organizing as a solution to some of these problems; in that session we described our efforts to organize a psychiatric day-care program. Most of this chapter will consist of the transcript of that class, which I've left intact for the most part. Before presenting it, however, I'd like to place things a bit more in context.

For some time now, radicals in the mental health field have been using their skills to provide "movement people" with direct services. Also, at least in Berkeley, we've been teaching others—mostly non-professionals—how to provide psychiatric help to each other and our allies. These services are increasingly being provided through "counter institutions"—rap centers, psychiatric emergency centers, free clinics, and so forth.

However, while our counter-institutions are important and must be nurtured, I do not see that they alone will insure the kind of thoroughgoing change needed for the health of this country. Nor is it economically possible or even necessarily attractive for most people to "drop out." In order to build the massive base which will be the ultimate guarantee of radical change in our society many people will have to create counter-movements within establishment institutions and agencies to gain control over them, thus taking power over the working conditions of their chosen occupation, which is one of the most basic needs of human life. The transcript of our discussion at the Free University shows how we tackled some of the many problems of self-determination and community control posed by establishment institutions—in this case, Contra Costa County Hospital in Martinez, California.

For example: a therapist whom everyone in the day-care program valued greatly had been told he would be fired because he hadn't met a certain civil service requirement. The requirement had to do with a technicality about credentials. Some of the patients brought up the subject in a community meeting; the possibility of losing one of the most effective and loved workers in the program made many people feel unhappy and helpless. Then one of us said, "Wait a sec. Maybe we don't have to take this flat on our backs." This bit of dynamite produced an avalanche of talk and determination in the patients to "take care of business." More community meetings were held, during which the politics of the situation, as well as people's experiences in it, were discussed.

These meetings encouraged a group of five or six patients plus a few staff people to make an intense argument at the civil service commission hearing. Most of the commission members were astonished to hear the community assert its right to keep the therapist on the staff. But they listened and we won.

If it's possible to separate the two notions, we won in political terms and also in therapeutic terms. Politically, what we won—and "we" means the patient-staff coalition—was not controlling power over the institution but a certain amount of influence, a veto power that would make it possible for us to determine the people we would work with. The therapeutic results were that the patients gained a heightened awareness of some of the forces that oppress them and valuable experience in working cooperatively to change an oppressive condition. Not only were they learning about external oppressive conditions, such as the ancient and totally useless civil service system, but in order to be effective at the civil service hearing these patients—who up until then had had precious little sense of their own potency—also had to fight against their internalized oppression (their images of themselves as crazy, impotent, invisible, unworthy). If acquiring the skills and strength to control the internal oppressor isn't a measure of growth or psychiatric success, I don't know what is.

It was an opening. We don't yet have a particularly clear image of what "the compleat take-over" of a hospital will look like. I only know that if one must work in an establishment institution, doing it with allies—with people who share the same visions—to gain power and control over our own lives is a more satisfying, more integrative experience than the one we've been taught to expect and accept.

THE TRANSCRIPT: A SUNDAY NIGHT IN BERKELEY, 1971

J.M.: If you were all here a couple of weeks ago, then you know that Claude [Steiner] announced that I'd be doing a rap on radical psychiatry and community organizing, with reference to my activity at Contra Costa County Hospital in Martinez. Well, I didn't do it alone out there. With me tonight are Danny Goldstine and Peter LaRiviere. Danny's a clinical psychologist at the hospital; Peter is a physician and also works out there. I'd like to point out that although Peter's an M.D., he's not a certified shrink. He's a good ole down-home radical psychiatrist, as is Danny. Now that I've introduced them, I'd like to outline for you some of the ideas we came up with working at the hospital, and then we can talk about how our ideas were applied.

One thing we've discovered is that, in certain situations, radical psychiatry might be construed as community organizing. We've discovered that the terms "radical psychiatry" and "community organizing" can be interchangeable; often (perhaps not often enough) the two functions intertwine. The only factor which would differentiate the two is the size of the groups. Let me explain. We begin with certain givens. You probably all know by now the formulas we use:

(1) Oppression + Mystification = Alienation

(2) Awareness + Contact = Liberation.[1]

[1] The second part of this formulation was later changed by members of the Radical Psychiatry Center. It now reads: Awareness + Contact = Action → Liberation.

STUDENT: Would you mind reviewing that? This is my first time here.

J.M.: Sure. O.K. The biggest problem that psychiatry must solve is alienation. Alienation is the sum of oppression plus mystification—not only are we oppressed, but we empower our oppression by lying to ourselves or believing the lies of others who deny we're oppressed or who say, "That's life, kid, you've just got to accept it." In the absence of oppression, people get along harmoniously with each other and with their environment. In order to achieve that harmonious state, to become free, we need awareness, contact, and action. Awareness alone isn't enough. Contact alone isn't enough. Action not supported by both is bound to be ineffective. Once we see we're oppressed—whether by the internalized oppressor (an often amorphous but insidious "It" which some of us call the Pig Parent) or by an external situation—we need each other, groups of each other, to confront and struggle against whatever oppresses us.

But these concepts, these formulas that I just mentioned, were initially conceived in the context of our problem-solving groups, which are generally limited to eight members and where the most intense focus is on internalized piggery. So we kept asking ourselves, "What new agonies will we perpetrate when our advocacy helps people overthrow internalized oppression if we don't also advocate fighting external oppression?"

Another way of stating the question is: "When people respond to a crazy world by going crazy, what are we really doing for those who seek our help when we elicit in them ways of seeing and acting which are 'different' from (if not entirely counter to) the established modes, when all of us (including me) must return to a world which is stark raving mad?"

Well, my answer is: "Unless we advocate and support radical social-political and economic change wherever and whenever possible we will not be doing much better than traditional psychiatry, we will be oppressors in support of the status quo." But in order to radically change our world we've got to do lots of organizing—in our case, that would mean creating alliances between health-care workers and the people they serve—and get other people excited about organizing. But instead of talking to you about the concepts, I think it would be a good idea to tell you what we actually did. I'm not quite sure how to proceed right now. I feel your attentiveness, and that really feels good to me, but I wonder if you have any questions.

STUDENT: Could you give me a historical perspective on this concept of radical psychiatry as community organizing?

P.L.: I got interested in the possibility of doing something specific with radical psychiatry when I was working as the guy who does the histories and physicals on the acute ward out there at the hospital. I found for the first time in my experience in medicine that though I was doing interesting work, I was feeling really oppressed; I was feeling just as oppressed as when I had been a medical student, and that was plenty oppressed. I knew something was wrong. I didn't know what the hell was wrong. I went to see the program chief in psychiatry. He's very sympathetic toward community psychiatry, but I think it's fair to say that he really hadn't found a way to effectuate his ideals. So when I talked to him and said I'd just had enough of J Ward, that I wasn't able to make any progress there, we were being opposed at every point in doing any therapy, much less radical therapy, he and I agreed that probably the best way to begin to do anything which would allow mental patients to determine things about their own lives, including their own therapy, was to work with what was then called the day-care program. This was then defined as a "day hospital" for people who, while they weren't locked up on J Ward or the other in-patient psychiatric ward, were really deeply alienated.

At that time, day-care was run by a woman, a social worker who did the usual traditional things with a group of say fifteen or sixteen people—outings, stringing beads, a little bit of therapy, stuff like that. And I began then to work with the program, alone at first, but quickly—as we began to discuss this in our radical psychiatry affinity group—other people got interested in what was happening. They began to come out and join in the effort, which has now resulted—not to get too much ahead of myself—in the formation of a psychiatric community which is partially self-determining and which is beginning to spread the practice of radical psychiatry into the general community.

STUDENT: You, Peter, mentioned that your feeling of being oppressed acting as a psychiatrist felt similar to your feelings of oppression as a medical student. Could you elaborate on that?

P.L.: Sure. Well, quite simply, I was not allowed to do what I was capable of doing. I was there to do a technical task, taking care of histories and physicals, which was ridiculously simple, with a group of people who had what were called acute psychiatric illnesses. It was the same as in medical school where I felt that my own skills would have been best employed in really finding out what was bothering people, rather than running lab tests. . . .

D.G.: I'd like to interject a point here relevant to Peter's feeling of oppression. It's so indicative of the kind of services that are delivered to psychiatric patients that hospital administrations would literally rather spend more time and money trying to get histories and physicals than they would on any attempt to do any kind of therapy. Here is a psychiatric setting, and they spend more time worrying about your ingrown toenails or your athlete's foot than they do trying to talk to you about what's really going on. At best they do a rather cursory talking to you, fill you up with medication, and write the discharge summary at the same time they do the initial interview.

STUDENT: Peter gave us a view of the program as it began through the hospital hierarchy. You were part of the hierarchy, Peter, and you had an "in." But what about Joy—how did you get involved?

J.M.: I guess it started when Peter would come to our Thursday night meetings and talk about what was going on at the hospital. I started going out to some planning sessions. Peter asked Danny and me and some other people to go to mental health planning meetings with him out at the hospital, kind of as consultants. He wanted us to talk about our experience at the rap center, because the rap center at its best was a good model of a community psychiatric center. At those planning meetings I sort of got turned on, but I was still very reluctant to get involved because the hospital atmosphere was so rigid. . . . I had been going down to J Ward on weekends with Danny and Peter, working with people who were having what gets labeled as "acute psychotic experience"—people who were either on acid or just having what the shrinks call "fresh breaks"; I saw them as people who were farther out than we are, or farther in, or in unusual states of consciousness. Anyway, we'd let Al Johnson, the head shrink on weekends, know when we'd be coming in; he'd pick out some people whom he'd judge as "appropriate" for Danny and me to work with, and then refrain from zonking them out—medicating them with the usual massive doses of phenothiazines. And though in some ways the experience was really rich for me and I think I helped some people, I didn't like working in an institution. I found it very oppressive.

On the other hand, I saw that I couldn't do radical psychiatry in a vacuum. That is, whether I was working with my groups in Berkeley or working with people on J Ward, I knew that so much of what was hurting people, myself included, had to do with what was going on with the world outside them. And when an opportunity presented itself to work in that "real" world, I simply couldn't turn my back on it. My strongest impulse was to get involved working with Peter to organize the day-care program. My status was "volunteer therapist." Peter and I co-led a therapy group. Nobody at the hospital knew anything about radical psychiatry, and at that early stage in the game I wasn't about to tip our hand. I was just "that strange-looking hippie woman who wore floor-length Indian dresses and no brassière, come to help out that doctor man who'd been commissioned by Leonti Thompson to change things. And Peter's a doctor, so he must know what he's doing; he certainly wouldn't bring in an incompetent therapist, even if she *does* dress kind of weird. . . ."

STUDENT: Joy, how did you view the hospital, how did it seem as a psychiatric or liberating situation? Did it have any of the elements that you perceive to be important in bringing about people's liberation?

J.M.: No. The first problem we were confronted with was the traditional hierarchy, with a male psychiatrist on top and a woman social worker under him. I think both of them freaked out under our pressure for community-patient participation. [Both of them left the hospital three or four months after we started.] I didn't see anything going on at the hospital that was liberating. Here, I'll read you an excerpt from a journal I started last summer, which may give you a feel for my experience of the hospital:

"It is a sterile, airless institutional green room. There are nine or ten men and one woman sitting around a long table talking.

"Peter and I walk in. I make eye contact with one man who sits at the head of the table. No one else seems to notice us. No one moves to make room for us at the table.

"But outside the circle of people rimming the table there are two chairs, against the wall.

"We sit close so our thighs and shoulders touch. I am aware of the integrity of my being, my sexuality, the beauty of my serene face, my relaxed graceful body, and how natural my body feels sitting close to Peter, whose face also is serene, whose body is also open, unselfconscious, naturally postured as a child —belly relaxed and round, breathing easy, thighs apart. . . .

"I look at the faces around the table. Their expressions go from bored to anxious to depressed to hostile to vacant or glassy-eyed.

"Sometimes someone says something sort of funny and sometimes someone laughs. Too hard. Nervously. The bodies of the people appear to be stiff-limbed, rigid, involuted. Living dead. These people are psychologists, psychoanalysts, psychiatrists, and psychiatric social workers. They're planning the lives of people they call The Mentally Ill."

You can imagine how awful, how poisonous that scene felt to me. I'd come from a very unstructured environment at the rap center, and here I walked into a place that was uptight, and had forms, and people had to write stuff in charts, and I wasn't into taking notes on people or stuff like that. . . . I came from a place where people had a lot of physical contact, where stroking was an important element of therapy, whether it was physical stroking or verbal, and I walked into the hospital where people didn't touch each other—either physically or emotionally. They had no permission to touch each other, there was very little real protection. The people were deceived into believing they were protected because they had the walls of the hospital around them, and the hierarchy with doctors around them, but there was nothing I could call growth-producing or liberating human experience. . . .

STUDENT: How did you ease these people out who couldn't cope with your trip, your way of therapy?

D.G.: They eased themselves out.

P.L.: What we did was to engage the patients in a group process that became too hot for the other staff people. There was a lot of shock value, I think, in the fact that Joy is a high school dropout, though eminently well-trained to do therapy, and that shocked the hell out of them. They were O.K. people, they just didn't like intensity. They didn't like really getting into things. So it wasn't like we marched in in a heavy Marxist-Leninist way and said "You're no good—out." It wasn't like that at all. We just made things more intense.

J.M.: They were running a finishing school,[2] as we got to call it, and they didn't dig our ideas about community control. We really wanted to work with the existing staff. We went there with an attitude of affiliating and not ripping anyone off or hurting anyone; and like Peter says, they just couldn't deal with it. The concept of a peer-group organization was just too heavy.

P.L.: Like for instance, we insisted right from the beginning that patients be allowed to attend all staff meetings, and that really freaked the staff.

STUDENT: How do you cope with the fact that it's a county hospital run by a board of directors? What happened with that?

---

[2] Now, some three-and-a-half years later, I'd call it "a finishing school for the powerless."—J.M.

D.G.: Well, having a really good boss has something to do with that. I mean the program chief is a very bright man, and he really wants to do something. He really wants to produce an atmosphere where people are going to get better. So he was willing to go along when we said we wanted patients to come to staff meetings; we don't believe in a system that doesn't include their participation. It's actually a very simple notion, but it's amazing just how the tone of things changes when it actually starts to happen. It doesn't matter how many come, or even if some days nobody comes—just plant the idea that one patient might walk in the door, and the whole way people conduct their business gets changed.

STUDENT: Do they come?

D.G.: Yes. By no means do all of them come, though I'd say around twenty percent show up at some of the staff meetings. But the idea is that you can't get away with all those mystifying trips. You can't say things like "this guy is a chronic undifferentiated schizophrenic."

STUDENT: I want to know how Danny got involved in this whole thing.

D.G.: I guess it started for me when I met Joy. I went to volunteer at the free clinic over a year ago and Joy interviewed me and decided that I was good enough to be her co-therapist. I had just returned from teaching at a very fancy women's school in the East . . . and I thought: "You've gone to school for fifteen years, and you've got a Ph.D. and you're O.K.," and here I was being interviewed by a high school dropout who decided that I was good enough to work with her. I dug Joy, I suppose more because of it than in spite of it. But I think I'd like to talk not only about how I got involved in the hospital thing, but also about how things like what we did can happen. And I'll call them principles of organizing, though they're hardly principles, just thoughts that might be helpful to other people.

To begin with, you have to have allies. So Peter told our affinity group, and we got together and rapped about such things. Joy and I resonated to what he was doing. So we would go out on weekends and do psychiatry with people on this understaffed ward. Why weekends? Weekends were a time when we had a friendly ally in charge. Well, he wasn't really an ally, but he was tolerant.

So another principle is: Have a tolerant or friendly psychiatrist in charge where you want to do your work. Also, on weekends, a lot of the heavy-number chiefs aren't there; so you'll have a lot more flexibility. If you wander around and open a locked door, no one's going to jump on top of you. Also, we were thought to be semi-experts. That is, we had long hair and stuff like that so we must know about drugs, right? And these people knew nothing about drugs. All they knew was that all these scared people were coming in and they didn't know how to relate to them.

So that's another principle: Demonstrate some expertise in a particular area so the various authorities will think they can somehow benefit from your presence. In our case, they looked on us not only as long-haired weirdo freaks but also as people who knew something that could benefit them. And when we went around opening locked doors and talking to people the staff didn't totally freak out. Another principle is: Let them think they are getting a good deal. In fact, they were. There were several of us coming out and working for nothing at that time, helping them perform a service that they were interested in having performed.

But things don't always happen miraculously. It didn't always run so smoothly. Sometimes we had hassles with nurses, we had hassles with the psychiatrist in charge of the ward, but we were polite and friendly. While we really didn't compromise our principles in any sense, or hesitate to do things that we thought were important, we *did* make a conscientious effort to learn people's names and say "hi" and be friendly, offer people a bite of our candy bar, hug each other in their presence. Just being warm, friendly people really did have an effect. As one might expect, some of the most oppressed people who worked on the ward responded to us most quickly. People like technicians, orderlies, aides didn't quite know what to make of us, but they kind of liked us; they were friendly toward us.

So one of the things that resulted was that we felt welcomed on that ward. We were adding to what existed. I'm not sure if that's completely honest. We would open locked wards. Now it turns out one of the reasons they always have locked wards is that all these places are always understaffed. They have all these loony crazy people wandering around causing trouble, singing songs and things of that sort . . . but if people whose job it is to keep order in all of that chaos see you as really trying to help them, they're a hell of a lot less offended by a fairly audacious act like opening a locked door. And if what you do doesn't work and you cop to it and take responsibility for it and say, "Gee, I guess it didn't work when we let Joe out and he ran away," or something like that, and you apologize and say, "I guess we'll have to work out a better system, but I really don't think social isolation is the proper way to treat this person's freak-out," then it becomes a common problem for everyone to solve, rather than a problem of simply establishing a smooth-running show on the ward. The transition from my volunteering on weekends to becoming a paid employee of the county was helped along immeasurably by the fact that they needed a psychologist. This is a touchy subject, and I wish I knew how to engineer such things because it's clear that unless you've discovered a new biological principle of how to live, you have to get paid for your services, and they tend to want to pay "professionals." We really do not have a properly organized principle of how to get hired at these institutions.

STUDENT: What other pressures, besides asking that patients be admitted to staff meetings, did you bring to bear on the people you were working with? What techniques did you use?

J.M.: Some of the most important work we did took place in community meetings . . . most hospitals' "community" meetings are phony, token events—pastimes—having little resemblance to political organizing, much less good psychiatry. Instead, they consist of a bunch of super-zombies (over-medicated and electroshocked patients) who have been herded into a circle where other less-than-super zombies (bored and depressed doctors) try to "analyze the group." The community meetings we insisted on having at Martinez were the exact opposite. While attendance was optional, patients wanted to go, they had real power and nobody was ever bored. In fact, community meetings were absolutely crucial to the life of the program. First, we would talk about *real* things, such as how to make the program work—meaning what to do so that people wouldn't need the program; we worked on getting people off medications, giving and getting strokes, getting meaningful work, setting up happy group living situations, dealing with oppressive hospital policies, and so on. Second, the meetings were divided into two categories, therapeutic and government. Third, *all* workers, not just the doctors, were encouraged to attend—they were needed. Fourth, while there were regularly scheduled meetings, one of each type per week, anyone could call additional meetings if needed. Fifth, staff did not always run meetings. Patients also took responsibility for facilitating.

In addition to community meetings, we instituted Contact raps, instead of the usual intake procedure. I never once wrote a word in anyone's chart. I refused. At every opportunity I criticized the charts and the garbage that was written in them. Sure enough, pretty soon patients were demanding to read their charts. I did a training group in radical psychiatry—at the request of eight of the patients—so patients could learn to lead groups.

D.G.: We pushed the idea of contracts pretty hard. You know: What do you want for yourself? What do you want from us? We would tell people that the oppression and screwed-upness in their lives led them to get into certain unhappy scenes, and that it wasn't our job to put them through a pretzel-making machine and send them back to the same shitwork that drove them crazy.

STUDENT: What kind of contracts did they make up?

J.M.: The same kind as Danny and I get in the group we do here in Berkeley. There's nothing magical about it. Contracts like "I want to get strokes"; "To move away from my parents"; "To stick up for myself"; "To get angry"; stuff like that. So, introducing contracts at the hospital was crucial, too. We introduced every principle and technique of radical psychiatry that we could; at first we used as little rhetoric as possible, except with a few people who could relate to it; and then eventually in big meetings, in the community meetings, other people began to pick up our language and, most important, the ideas behind it.

D.G.: Some of the most oppressed people in mental hospitals are not the patients, but the staff. For example, even nurses, who have some status—because they're not like techs or orderlies—stand up every time a doctor walks into the room. And the nurses frequently got pretty hostile when they saw us with our long hair and heard us talking about liberation. But lately we've been approached by the head of the psychiatric nursing staff to train all her people, herself included, to use radical psychiatry.

STUDENT: I have a friend who's a psychiatrist in a day treatment center in the city and he's definitely a prisoner. He's tried to do things and the reactions he gets are yes, yes, and then nothing gets done. It's driven him crazy—now *he* has to see a psychiatrist!

D.G.: You have to have allies or you will go crazy. That's what Contact is all about.

STUDENT: Well, how do you get the word to people about how to go about doing this in other hospitals? I mean, if other workers don't really know there's been a success, they just feel they're beating their heads against the wall. What can you do to get these other hospitals to get the same thing going somewhere else?

J.M.: Well, one thing we're doing is taping this class so I can do up an article for *The Radical Therapist,* which you could refer your friend to. Also, I think your friend might do well to get involved at the Radical Psychiatry Center here in Berkeley. . . .

P.L.: If you're in a situation like that, like the one your friend's in, you've got to get out—which is what I would have done, except that I found Joy and Danny. And I guess the three of us were like a critical mass, because when we started there were only two other people on the whole staff. Anyone who came in after that, after we started working there, found we were more fun to relate to and had this new idea they were open to, and it got bigger and bigger until the other two left. With a critical mass of people saying, "It's O.K., it's O.K. to make changes," everything goes fine. If you really get into permission with one another, it's very powerful. . . .

J.M.: Yes, we used permission techniques and the concept of permission. We told people they had options. We showed people alternatives. But I think it's important to add here that when leaders go around telling people it's O.K. to change, they must also guarantee protection. I mean that whether you're "doing a therapy group" or organizing a community, it's part of your responsibility to stay with and support the people you've succeeded in turning on, until they become self-supporting. Otherwise, the whole thing becomes a cruel joke. Psychiatric interns and residents do this to ward patients all the time: they come in—lone saviors—try new innovations, offer hope, then duck out when they've "done their time."

When people get to a point in their lives where they've decided to change their death scripts to life scripts, life often gets plenty scary. It's at that point that protection—the reassurance that everything's going to be O.K.—is crucial. That reassurance can be transmitted directly and verbally. It is also communicated, often quite dramatically, by example. Though certainly there were times when Danny, Peter, and I were down, or anxious—getting impatient with waiting for the changes we wanted in the program—we never had any doubt that what we were demanding was right on.

We were always confident that the values we struggled to give expression to—self-determination, community control, loving human relationships—were values that we have a right to pursue because we are human beings. That was also a kind of protection. We had each other for protection—at the hospital and in our affinity group in Berkeley—and so we were able to show others what we meant when we opposed the idea of individualistic solutions like long-term one-to-one therapy or one-to-one political manipulation, and when we talked about Contact and the protection that comes from working with peers in a group.

I can't stress enough that any attempt to organize, or even just to raise consciousness a bit, without the guaranteed protection of allies, is doomed to fail. Lenny Bruce, one of the greatest artists and political commentators of our time, tried to do it alone. He had no protection. Lenny Bruce was suicided by society.

SUMMARY (by Joy Marcus)

*Radical psychiatry and community organizing are interchangeable in their practice.

*The basic theories and techniques of radical psychiatry can be transferred to broader political arenas than therapy groups.

* Just as in effective psychiatry, effective political action requires that people feel permission to: 1) define problems—see, think, feel; 2) be angry; 3) fight back; 4) have vision, use imagination, have fun; 5) work cooperatively; 6) organize; and 7) follow-through.

*Being engaged in a community organizing process is therapeutic for people; in order to take political power we need to rid ourselves of internalized oppression; while being engaged in the process of taking power, we feel more alive and are able to experience ourselves as intelligent and powerful, thus ridding ourselves of old "tapes" about being "crazy," "stupid," "worthless," "weak," "incompetent."

*Effective political action is a good indicator of psychiatric success.

*The most pleasurable kind of organizing occurs when people act in behalf of their own liberation, rather than entering a situation from a markedly one-up (and guilty) position to "Rescue" an oppressed class.

10. RADICAL PSYCHIATRY HISTORY

by Claude Steiner

THE THEORY

The theory of Radical Psychiatry was conceived early in 1969 when I began teaching a course by that name at the Free University in Berkeley. At that time it consisted simply of a series of complaints against establishment psychiatry which had been written into a Manifesto on the occasion of the 1969 annual convention of the American Psychiatric Association in San Francisco, and offered few theoretical or practical alternatives to the oppressive conditions of establishment psychiatry of the times. In the summer of 1969 on the heels of the People's Park uprising in Berkeley, a Free Clinic was established by the medics who had assisted the injured and wounded in the Berkeley streets. Part of the Free Clinic's plan was to include psychological counseling; and a few months after the Free Clinic opened its doors a Rap ("Radical Approach to Psychiatry") Center was started, with welfare and draft interviews, contact rap, street rap, problem solving groups, and a training program.

In the context of the Rap Center's activities, the theory began to develop. I contributed my understanding of group psychotherapy, transactional analysis, and psychiatry in general. Hogie Wyckoff brought with her feminism, radical politics, and Marxist theory. Joy Marcus, also a radical feminist, contributed community organizing theory and skills and poetry. Many others contributed with their criticisms, their struggles, and further theory. Ronald Laing's, Herbert Marcuse's, and Wilhelm Reich's thought became clearly relevant and were adapted into the theory. The theory became a blend of political and psychiatric thought which became applicable to the everyday problems in people's lives. As more people joined the radical psychiatry movement, the theory was applied not only in problem-solving groups but also in their daily lives. Over the next four years sexism, the oppressiveness of monogamy, hetero-sexual and family structures, competition, the uses and abuses of power, affinity and enmity became the focus of the theory resulting in further theory about relationships, cooperation, and power.

At approximately the time when we started working at the Rap Center (spring, 1970), Michael Glenn, a psychiatrist in the Air Force stationed in Minot, North Dakota, and a small group of people started the quarterly journal, *The Radical Therapist,* which from its second issue included writings from the radical psychiatrists in Berkeley. Eventually, one whole issue of *The Radical Therapist* (November, 1971) was devoted to the writing from radical psychiatry. This book is a selection of articles from that issue. At the same time, Michael Glenn and the other members of the R.T. Collective moved to Cambridge, Massachusetts and in April, 1972 *The Radical Therapist* changed its name to *Rough Times.*

The change of name was the outcome of a struggle within the R.T. Collective between therapists and radical theoreticians who opined that doing therapy and teaching therapy skills are activities which ultimately oppress people. The new name, *Rough Times,* announced their intentions to concentrate on documenting and attacking the oppressive activities of psychiatrists and allied oppressive institutions.

In January, 1973, a group of radical psychiatrists in Berkeley, including Hogie Wyckoff, Joy Marcus, and myself, started a new journal named *Issues in Radical Therapy* which pursued the editorial goals of the original *Radical Therapist*. This journal (Box 23544, Oakland, California 94623) continues to publish theoretical and practical articles about therapy and radical psychiatry and is now in its second year of publication.

THE BERKELEY RADICAL PSYCHIATRY CENTER (BRPC)

The BRPC had its beginning with a small core of people at the Free Clinic's Rap Center who considered themselves radical psychiatrists. Radical psychiatrists were in the minority at the Rap Center and over a period of time eventually ran into difficulties with the rest of the workers.

On the one hand, the "professionals" became alarmed at the radical anti-establishment psychiatric notions of radical psychiatrists and the increasing trend toward linking psychology and politics and toward revolutionary involvement by radical psychiatrists.

On the other hand, a leveling trend was introduced by counter-culture persons who felt that all hierarchies in an organization should be abolished and who felt that no one was especially knowledgeable or capable in the field of psychiatry, so that no approaches were correct but rather everyone should "do their thing" according to their interests and inclinations. This group reacted against radical psychiatrists, accusing them of being authoritarian and elitist.

A third area from which radical psychiatry was attacked was by persons in movement politics who found fault with radical psychiatrists' points of view on the basis of the intolerant "Lefter Than Thou" criticism (see Chapter 15). This criticism, largely theoretical, discounted the work of radical psychiatrists on the basis of not being sufficiently revolutionary or radical. The Rap Center's business meetings, which were operated by the consensus of anyone who attended, became more and more polemical, less and less effective, and eventually so extraordinarily frustrating that almost no decisions of any significance could be made and only the most banal matters could be discussed and acted upon.

Because of this, the radical psychiatry group had asked to become a separate part of the Berkeley Community Health Project, on equal status with the Rap Center and the Free Clinic. This status was temporarily given; and as radical psychiatry developed further, free now of the different lines of attack upon it, the conflict over its principles and practice grew, and eventually in late 1970 the radical psychiatry group was asked to leave the Berkeley Community Health Project. A few months later the group found a house at 2333 Webster, and with its own space and headquarters began to work hard at its tasks. In a year's time, the Radical Psychiatry Center had grown by leaps and bounds, daily contact raps were held which were heavily attended, a large waiting list for people who wanted to join problem-solving groups developed, about fifty people received training and eventually joined the center as facilitators, and a very well-attended Radical Psychiatry Conference was held in the summer of 1971. (See Chapter 11 for a description of the Center's operation at that time.)

The summer of 1971 was the high point of spirit and enthusiasm at the Radical Psychiatry Center. Everything seemed positive and constructive; it appeared as if the radical psychiatry movement was headed for continuing expansion and growth. Three communal houses had been established in which radical psychiatrists attempted to live by radical psychiatry principles; training programs in Los Angeles, San Francisco, and Sacramento were being held; it appeared that other Radical Psychiatry Centers would be started; and, judging by the positive reception of people plus the great enthusiasm of the workers, it seemed that the radical psychiatry movement would continue to flourish.

However, a split developed within the radical psychiatry community at this point. A group of facilitators who were unhappy about the conditions at the Center held a series of secret meetings in which they discussed important and often valid criticisms of the radical psychiatry community. The secret nature of these meetings was an unexpected violation of the assumptions of cooperation and honesty which were assumed to govern behavior within the community. Until this secret surfaced, unresolved bad feelings and paranoias ran rampant and work in action rap and collective suffered. The new radical psychiatry group was composed of people who felt oppressed within the community. An open meeting was held in which the new group criticized the workings of the Radical Psychiatry Center (see Appendix at the end of the book); following this, the community split into two camps: the New Radical Psychiatry group (comprising about twenty group leaders, most of whom had recently joined the Center); and about thirty others (among them Joy Marcus, Hogie Wyckoff, and myself) who refused to continue to work with the members of the New Radical Psychiatry group.

The split was complete by the fall of 1972, and a struggle ensued over the rights that the two groups had over the house on Webster Street in which the Radical Psychiatry Center operated. The new group wanted to use the house on certain days; the old group did not want to share the house with them. In the end, the house, owned by me, was locked up by us, and both groups had to find other quarters to pursue their activities. In time, the old Radical Psychiatry Center group returned to the house.

The split in radical psychiatry badly weakened what had appeared to be a strong, positive movement. Within the next year, the three original members of the Radical Psychiatry Center—again Joy Marcus, Hogie Wyckoff, and myself—left the Center one after the other, at different times and for different reasons. At the present time, the future of the group is uncertain as to its political and psychiatric directions. Only time can tell what their impact in the radical psychiatry and radical therapy movements will be.

11. AN ANALYSIS OF THE STRUCTURE OF THE BERKELEY RADICAL PSYCHIATRY CENTER (FALL, 1972)

by Members of the Radical Psychiatry Center[1]

The Berkeley Radical Psychiatry Center (BRPC) is a community psychiatry organization with headquarters at 2333 Webster, Berkeley, California 14705. We serve people living in Berkeley and North Oakland.

INTRODUCTION

The BRPC is presently made up of five training collectives, the group members' organization, the Rap press work collective, IRT, a political study group, and problem-solving groups for leaders.

ACTION RAP

The BRPC is open to the public Monday through Friday from 5:30 to 7:30 for Action Rap which is a

[1] The principal authors of this chapter (as well as Chapters 12 and 13) are Anita Friedman, Claude Steiner, and Hogie Wyckoff.

drop-in group facilitated by members of each day's training collective.

The Action Rap (formerly called Contact Rap) is overseen by the Head, who is a member of that day's training collective. The Head is responsible for it that day, and is expected to be available to make on-the-spot decisions in extreme situations such as suicide risk, violent behavior, drug overdoses, or any acute psychiatric emergency that may occur. The Head makes certain that Action Rap is a protected situation and that there is a facilitator in each room.

Various things that can happen at Action Rap are: a) people can get information about radical psychiatry; b) people in need of help can sign up for groups and work in Action Rap while on the waiting list; c) people in crisis can get emergency help; and d) people can get strokes. By strokes we mean positive human recognition and contact. People can work in the social context of Action Rap to break down the artificial constraints on people's freedom to love each other (stroke economy) by giving strokes, asking for strokes, accepting strokes that they want, rejecting strokes that they don't want, and by stroking themselves.

We ask people not to come more than twice a week. (We specified this limit because we were overcrowded and weren't able to take care of everyone.) We ask people for contributions to support the BRPC.

The Action Rap usually adheres to the following format:

It starts with an introductory explanation in one central room. The group then divides into different rooms. The general contract is to learn how to overcome our own and each others' mystified oppression. Hopefully, there are not more than fifteen people in each room, preferably ten. We sometimes make contracts, which are work agreements, to do problem-solving in specific areas. In each room at least one group leader acts as a facilitator and gives political and problem-solving information. The facilitator helps people meet each other and creates safety by not letting people verbally or physically attack each other and helps people ask for and get what they want. It is not the facilitator's responsibility to Rescue people in this situation. By Rescue we mean assuming more than half the responsibility for people getting what they want. The general working agreement in radical psychiatry is that we offer options and help people get in touch with what they want so that they can work to get it. It is important to remember that people who are in a psychiatric crisis always take priority, and facilitators should call on the Head in any emergency situation.

The Action Rap is the hub of the BRPC's activities. It takes the place of the intake or screening interview of most psychiatric facilities and gives the newcomer an opportunity to evaluate the BRPC before making any commitment. From Action Rap a person may sign up for and proceed to a problem-solving group or, when necessary, to a one-to-one crisis intervention session.

PROBLEM-SOLVING GROUPS

A major psychiatric activity of the BRPC is problem-solving groups. We solve problems in groups instead of in individual therapy because we feel that teaching people to act collectively is a vital part of our work as community organizers. Problem-solving groups are co-led by two trained radical psychiatrists. The group is made up of eight people who are seeking help. Two observers from training collectives may also be present to learn how a problem-solving group functions and to exchange feedback with the leaders. Their relationship with the group members parallels that of the group leaders in that they do not play with group members while observing/leading the group.

The group work is based on the Principles, Manifesto, and Working Contract of the BRPC. The following are specifics of how we work:

All group members make a contract with the leaders and the group as to what they want to accomplish. The contract should be a simple positive statement that could be easily understood by an eight-year-old.

It is expected that people attend regularly. The group starts and ends on time. People are expected to call ahead if they can't attend. If a person doesn't contact the group for two weeks in a row she or he is no longer considered a member of the group. People are expected to come to group drug-free. This includes psychotropic drugs such as Librium, Elavil, Thorazine, heroin, alcohol, marijuana, etc. However, a reasonable and safe time will be allowed for withdrawal when needed, usually a maximum of a month. If at the time of the meeting a group member is under the influence of a drug, she or he is still expected to attend; however, under these circumstances she or he may be asked not to take up time with ineffectual attempts at work.

People usually sign up to work when they come into group and circle their name if they are in special need. It is the group's responsibility to keep track of time and be sure that everyone gets what they want. If, during the week, people are in trouble they can call other group members or the group leaders for support or information. Through our experience we have found that it interferes with problem-solving when group leaders have sexual or intense social contact with group members. We prefer that members of the same problem-solving group don't have sexual contact because it may make it impossible for them to work in the same group together.

People who join a radical psychiatry problem-solving group while in therapy elsewhere are given one month to choose one or the other. We are unwilling to work with people using other psychiatric services with the exception of body therapies because: a) it is often a contradiction in terms of approach to problems; b) it is a duplication of service in a situation where there exists a scarcity; and c) our experience shows us that it is a difficult working situation.

It is the responsibility of group members to support the center financially but how they do it is up to them.

TRAINING COLLECTIVES

There are five training collectives in radical psychiatry. Each is made up of a maximum of eight radical psychiatrists. Initially, the training collective is led by a radical psychiatrist capable of training others, the goal being for everyone to eventually have equal information, responsibility, and power.

When a training collective achieves information and skills in how to lead problem-solving groups, the leader begins to bring problems from her problem-solving group to the collective to facilitate the process of becoming an equal member. Thus, everyone takes equal responsibility for leadership; and the training group becomes a collective without a designated leader.

The responsibilities of a training collective are: a) supervision and work at the Action Rap of the day; b) training group leaders by the exchange of information, observing each others' groups, self-evaluation, asking for and giving honest feedback and supporting each other; c) actively taking responsibility for all the groups coming out of that collective; and d) participation in and responsiveness to the planning group, and other

BRPC community activities such as Sunday Seminar and Phase II.

People interested in training are advised to go to the different Action Raps to meet the members of the various collectives. New trainees are admitted to preliminary training based on consensus of the training collective. New people in training and radical psychiatrists from the collective work together for at least four weeks in Action Rap. Every session is followed by an exchange of information and feedback. Then people in preliminary training work in the training collective for another four weeks, after which time everyone decides if they feel good about continuing to work together.

TEACHERS' COLLECTIVE

The teachers' collective is made up of the leaders of each training collective and others involved in teaching radical psychiatry. The contract is to learn to teach radical psychiatry and to ask for and give honest feedback about each others' work. Leaders bring problems and information about their collectives to it. When there is no longer a need for a leader in a training collective, its members will send a chosen representative to the teacher's collective.

This is how a training collective looks in action:

One person volunteers to facilitate that meeting. He writes the agenda on a blackboard so everyone can see what needs to be covered. This facilitator then helps the group keep track of the time and works to help the meeting run smoothly.

Based on our experience, we have found that groups work best if people unload held resentments and paranoid fantasies at the beginning of the meeting. After the work of the meeting is completed it is important to leave time for a self-conscious discussion of how people worked together as a group and to exchange feedback and strokes that have not yet been given.

PLANNING GROUP[2]

The planning group is the final decision and policy making body of the radical psychiatry community. It serves to get community-wide consensus on proposals generated in the various collectives. The Center's activities are planned at the bi-weekly meeting. The planning group is composed of two representatives from each work collective and two representatives from the group members' organization. Anyone in a radical psychiatry group or in radical psychiatry training may attend planning group meetings. However, only representatives will have a voice at these meetings. The agenda and minutes of the planning group will be available to anyone who wishes to read them, and representatives of the different groups are expected to post agenda items ahead of the meeting so that those attending will be prepared to deal with them. Decisions of the planning group are hopefully reached by consensus; but in the case of an item that is hotly disputed, the majority vote will carry. Majority and minority opinions will be duly recorded in the minutes. Planning group decisions are taken back to the different groups represented, and the vote of the representatives will be ratified by the whole group. If dissatisfaction with either the vote of the group representative or the total vote is encountered, the matter will be re-opened upon request.

THE SUNDAY NIGHT SEMINAR is a forum for political

[2] Planning Group was later replaced by a General Community Meeting held every other Sunday. Proposals were passed by consensus vote, with three "nays" constituting veto power.

and theoretical discussion. It is open only to people in training and their invited guests. This is a good place for people from different collectives to meet each other and exchange information. This forum is open to any interested individual or group. The seminar is led by a facilitator and decisions about scheduling future presentations and discussions are made there. Group members who are invited are asked to consult with their leaders and observers.

PHASE II is a collective of group leaders which concerns itself with the relationships of the BRPC to geographical areas other than our community. It meets weekly and takes its proposals to the planning group.

The group members' organization meets periodically and brings its proposals to the planning group.

ACCESS TO MEETINGS

Action Rap is open to all. Problem-solving groups are closed. Phase II, training collectives, and teacher's collective are open to all persons in training by arrangement.

Planning group is open to group members and leaders in training; anyone else interested may ask to attend. Sunday seminars are open to persons in training and their invited guests. All other community meetings are open to group members unless specified.

12. A WORKING CONTRACT FOR GROUP LEADERS AT THE BERKELEY RADICAL PSYCHIATRY CENTER

1. We believe that in order for Radical Psychiatry to remain relevant and viable it must be open to new ideas and change. All values, theory, and practice, including this contract, are subject to a dialectical process of change based on an ongoing and cooperative dialogue.

2. We are a center serving the psychiatric needs of the Berkeley community in which we live (i.e., people within Berkeley and North Oakland). Our primary interest is in organizing our community, and we consider its needs our first priority. We see ourselves as a "community" center, where we provide for one of our own basic needs.

3. We act as community organizers; that is, we teach problem-solving skills and support people to collectively reclaim political power. We see political power as power to control our own lives and environment.

4. We believe that all our actions are political and that it is not possible to separate our "personal" from our "political" lives. We believe that people have the right to direct their own lives; to assert this right is to use political power. We believe that isolated individuals cannot successfully eliminate their oppression and that there

are no personal solutions possible to political oppression.

5. We are committed to struggle against all unequal and oppressive power relationships. We see ourselves as a part of a larger revolutionary struggle for human liberation.

6. We succeed through collectivity and affinity. We believe that cooperation is essential to our collective strength; we work with people with whom we feel safety and affinity.

7. We communicate radical political values. We believe that in this society people are oppressed. When internalized, this oppression becomes "mental illness." Radical psychiatry makes clear the connection between external oppression and psychiatric disturbance.

8. Throughout our training we take an active part in shaping all our information and skills with each other. We work with a co-leader, take observers into our training collectives and problem-solving groups, and we train others in radical psychiatry.

9. We fulfill the minimum time commitment to radical psychiatry by working in Action Rap at least once a week, by working in a training collective, and by leading groups for at least one year.

10. We acknowledge that there are standards of what is good radical psychiatry. These standards are determined by training collectives. We value problem-solving skills. We achieve these skills by working cooperatively and by committing ourselves to ask for and give honest criticism, feedback, and support from each other and group members.

11. In our work we use contracts which are cooperative work agreements, so that people ask for what they want and work to get it.

12. We work to eliminate power imbalances and equalize power among all people in the radical psychiatry community.

13. Our reward in doing and training others to do problem-solving groups is to see people reclaim their political power and to become active with us in creating social changes. We don't do radical psychiatry for strokes or money from group members.

We don't do problem-solving with people who are in other types of therapy (with the exception of some types of body work), because of scarcity of services and contradictions in theory and practice.

Our experience has taught us that sexual or intense social contact with group members impairs the work of problem-solving groups. We also avoid sexual contact with co-leaders, with the exception of already established relationships.

14. We affirm the Principles and Manifesto of Radical Psychiatry and this Contract in our work. We endeavor to remove the contradictions between radical psychiatry theory and our lives. We actively support the existence of the Berkeley Radical Psychiatry Center.

13. AN ANALYSIS OF THE POLITICAL VALUES OF THE BERKELEY RADICAL PSYCHIATRY CENTER

1. Liberation within an oppressive society is not possible. It is a mystification. People cannot be truly free if this society is not free because social oppression will necessarily impinge on their freedom.

2. We believe that people are by nature unwilling to oppress or be oppressed. The desire for liberation and the energy for the attainment of liberation comes from people's basic nature.

3. We believe that people's problems are political problems. Therefore, we teach radical political values as an integral part of problem-solving. However, we don't encourage people to do things they don't want to do. We use contracts so that they can freely define and ask for the help they want.

4. We don't rescue people. The way out of oppression is to decide to do something about it and act on that decision. Action means work, not the passive consumption of a radical psychiatrist's efforts and skills. The necessity for action is an integral part of radical psychiatry awareness.

5. We support people to take back their power as autonomous human beings. Our goal is to empower people

and to de-empower leadership. We teach people problem-solving skills so that they can learn how to bring about revolutionary change through action. We don't promote pacification and adjustment to the status quo by merely providing people with short-term comfort and good feelings.

6. Alienation = Oppression + Mystification. People are alienated because power over their own lives has been taken away from them in the service of oppression. People internalize oppression by believing that the problem is within them rather than in an exploitative, elitist, and capitalist society, whose interest is in maintaining an alienated and docile population.

7. Oppression + Awareness = Anger. We demystify oppression and give people permission and support to use their emerging anger constructively to fight it—not just oppression which has been internalized but also oppression from the external world.

8. Contact + Awareness = Action → Liberation. Awareness here means radical awareness of political problems. Techniques such as gestalt therapy, transactional analysis, psychodrama, or role-playing do not directly demystify how people are oppressed. These techniques alone can in fact co-opt people's anger and be used in liberal pacification programs by providing contact without awareness or action. Our actions are designed to create stresses within the Psychiatric Establishment, not to relieve it by peaceful coexistence.

9. Unequal distribution of power, wherever found, is a source of oppression. We support those who are in a position of lesser power to become strong.

10. Sex roles oppress all people, especially women. In our society the nuclear family is used as a means of instilling oppressive values. In it children are mystified

and programmed to accept oppression, women are an unpaid labor force at home serving men who serve, in turn, as a production force for the profit of others. Monogamy promotes scarcity of strokes, which perpetuates isolation and alienation and encourages the consumption of "goods."

11. A radical psychiatrist is not merely a counterculture shrink. We are community organizers. We teach people problem-solving and the value of working together to reclaim their power.

12. Radical psychiatry is free. It is not a product for people to buy because we feel it is wrong to sell people back their humanness. We want to avoid being co-opted and corrupted as a commodity. We wish to provide radical psychiatrists with the means for support from sources other than fees for service from group members.

14. RADICAL PSYCHIATRY AND THE VIETNAM VETERAN by Robert Schwebel

Leading a radical psychiatry group of hospitalized veterans of the Vietnam War helped me understand the devastating effects of imperialist wars on the troops of the aggressors. It also helped me understand more about the nature of psychiatric problems and their remedies.

PSYCHIATRIC DISTRESS FITS THE SITUATION

The psychiatric distress of veterans of the United States military in Vietnam follows plainly and obviously from the experiences of those men. Large numbers of American soldiers were drafted, often against their will. Others, not given the facts, were convinced that they would be fighting for freedom and their brothers and sisters, so they enlisted. Once inducted, soldiers are given the basic messages: "Kill or get killed" and "Don't think and don't feel." American soldiers are taught to risk their lives and ordered to commit crimes against the Vietnamese people. At the gut level, many of these soldiers know there is something wrong with what has happened to them and with what they are doing. Of those that have this intuition or understanding, many become "mentally ill." It is not surprising that because they are either tricked or forced to get into the military, because they are ordered into dangerous situations, and because they are being shot at, many Vietnam veterans arrive in mental hospitals feeling "paranoid"—as if everyone is after them. It is also not surprising that because they have been involved in criminal and dehumanizing activities other Vietnam veterans arrive in hospitals feeling depressed, considering themselves worthless people not entitled to any human emotions and pleasures. It's a vicious circle: people who fear they are no good fear that other people are "out to get them"; and people who fear that other people are "out to get them" fear that they are no good. In all cases, the veterans end up feeling alienated from life and lonely and uneasy. "Mental patients" returning from the war in Vietnam end up hating themselves and hating other people. Just as by understanding their experiences their problems can be understood, so it is that by knowing their problems that their experiences can be understood. One veteran said, "I can't look anyone in the face anymore. I'd rather have come home in a box." Another veteran felt that he had become so ugly in Vietnam that he couldn't bear looking at himself in the mirror anymore.

All paranoia has a basis in reality. Sometimes it is easy to find the basis. For example, there was a twenty-two-year-old soldier who was tripping on acid with four "buddies." Two of them turned out to be police, and they handed him over to the authorities. Instead of arresting him, the authorities demanded that he inform on his friends. When he refused to do this, they made it look like he was informing anyway by having him report to them on a weekly basis so that everyone would notice. Soon his friends thought he was an informer. He became paranoid.

Another veteran became paranoid when he bought a

houseful of furniture on credit from a slick salesman who tricked him. As the terms of the contract unfolded he found himself spiraling into debt. He fell behind on many payments. Soon his phone service was about to be shut off, his car was repossessed, his rent was overdue, threatening lawyers were calling almost daily, and his furniture was about to be taken back.

The person who feels that he doesn't deserve to feel human emotions and pleasures knows that he has been involved in dehumanizing activities. People know when they are doing really bad things. A U.S. soldier was sitting alone in the jungle when he heard a noise in a tree. He turned around and shot into the tree as he had been trained to do, and an eight-year-old child fell down, dead. The young soldier stopped feeling emotions after that.

THE VIETNAM VETERAN AND RADICAL PSYCHIATRY

The military says, "Don't think and don't feel." Without exception, Vietnam veterans have good reason to think and feel that people have been after them and that they have been doing criminal and dehumanizing things. However, most G.I.'s return to civilian life ignoring what they have done and fitting in well in this society. Their ability to love and think is probably severely impaired as a result of their experiences which they must block out. The others—the ones who are overtly bleeding emotionally—are on to something. The Vietnam veteran who is paranoid knows that everyone is after him. The Vietnam veteran who does not have any emotions knows he has done wrong. In most hospital situations there is an attempt made to make people emotionally and intellectually discount their experiences or accept them uncritically. Quite possibly this is why distressed hospital patients often return to hospitals after an apparent recovery. Humans who know something about themselves are reluctant to give up this knowledge. In radical psychiatry groups we do not try to make veterans (or any group members) ignore or forget their experiences. We also don't try to "pig" (put down or attack) people and make them feel guilty. Rather, in a radical psychiatry group we build from an individual's knowledge and feelings and give them a chance to think and love more than they have been doing.

The basic principle of radical psychiatry is that all problems of a psychiatric nature are caused by mystified oppression. Mystified oppression makes people feel alienated. To combat alienation radical psychiatry gets people in contact with one another. To combat mystification radical psychiatry gets people aware of their oppression. And, to combat oppression, radical psychiatry gets aware people together.

AWARENESS AND THE VIETNAM VETERAN

It is very clear that Vietnam veterans have injunctions against thinking, especially about the ways in which they have been oppressed. In order for people to think and talk about things, a safe atmosphere had to be established. The stroke economy was loosened up by doing permission exercises which brought about stroking (giving human recognition and warmth, as defined by Eric Berne). Protection was provided by not permitting "pigging" and "trashing" (group pigging), so that people felt like they could say what they wanted to without fearing attack. Then, certain clear statements were made to the group: "It is O.K. to talk honestly about your own actual experiences," "It is O.K. to talk about how you feel," "It is O.K. to consciously choose your values," "It is O.K. to be scared," "Your gut feelings count," "Your gut intuitions count."

It is amazing how blind people are to really seeing the forces that oppress them. It is exciting to see how quickly, given a chance, they tune in to them. Aside from the individual and unique experiences of the veterans (which we dealt with in group), a common basis for paranoia was found throughout the group. First the draft (not to mention parents and school) and then their commanding officers ruled over the veterans by force. People whom they had trusted turned out to be against them: recruiters with great promises, teachers who told them it would be for freedom, officers who said it would be for their country, parents who said be brave for us, and friends who let them go. And—although they were not oppressed by the Viet Cong—those bullets that flew overhead were real. The oppression that got them into the service and the combat fears of everyday life in the war are what got these men doing the awful things they did. While they had some realization of what they did, they had little or no understanding of how they arrived at doing it.

Leading a group of Vietnam veterans shows the strong injunctions people have against really seeing the ways in which they are oppressed. People with no human pleasures or feelings stay that way because they don't believe they deserve any "goodies." They are aware of what they have done, but not of the ways in which they have been oppressed into doing these things. "Paranoid" people think everyone is after them; and, ironically, this prevents them from clearly figuring out who is oppressing them and zeroing in on that person. However, given an opportunity, people can come to understand the oppressive forces that shape their lives.

The blindness to oppression of the Vietnam veteran has a long history of development. Often, parents teach it to their children. Here are a few examples of how it works:

Two parents have just explained to their kid that she must do all the chores they assign. They have made it clear that she is to be "on duty" continually and subject to the whims, schedule, and needs of her parents regardless of her own needs, etc. The conversation continues:

PARENTS: Be good, my little girl, and do what I tell you. (Don't think about it. Good girls don't think.)

KID: I won't do it. (I know oppression when I see it.)

PARENTS: But what I say is in your best interest. You must listen to your parents (i.e., you don't *know*, I do).

KID: I will choose myself.

PARENTS: We love children who do as they are told. (I'll withdraw my love if you are not dependent on me and don't follow my rules. If you think for yourself, you lose my love.)

KID: I'll make up my own mind.

PARENTS: We are doing our best to be good parents. You should love your parents. (Here is something to fog up your mind. "Loving your parents" means doing exactly as they say. Love is obedience.)

Another example occurs when a young child sends out her radar, and observes oppressive behavior. For example, one parent puts down the other parent. The child protests, and the parents respond like this: "You're not being paid to think around here. This is not the concern of young children." (In other words, "Dummy up!") School is yet another institution that teaches blindness to oppression. At the same time as kids are oppressed in the classroom, they are taught about a world which exists without oppression.

CONTACT AND THE VIETNAM VETERAN

Along with increased awareness, the group provides an opportunity for emotional contact. In the group, people get together and stop hating themselves and hating other people.

Probably the most remarkable thing about the group making contact was the utter state of stroke starvation that the men suffered from. They gave and received few strokes. Yet, they easily learned to do stroke/permission exercises and benefited greatly from them. In one exercise developed by Claude Steiner a free stroke economy is proclaimed. Everyone is free to ask for, accept, offer, reject, or decline to give strokes. In a related exercise, called "Trash the Stroke Economy," developed by a training group collective in radical psychiatry, a circle is formed and one person at a time goes into the center. That person is free to ask for or offer to give strokes to anyone. People on the outside are free to reject or accept strokes and give or decline to give strokes when asked. The stroke starvation was so severe among the veterans that we often started meetings by doing back rubs for one another. When one new group member heard about the back rubs he said, "I don't want people walking all over me and pounding on me." However, this typically hard veneer was covering a very needy person who soon readily accepted strokes. This is often the case with Vietnam veterans.

TRASH AUTHORITY: AN EXERCISE

Most veterans suffered from the authoritarian control they lived under in the military. A fear of authority and an accompanying rigidness was not uncommon. Because they often had not had an opportunity to be on their own, many veterans still relied on their families. Few of the veterans had had an opportunity to choose their own values.

I developed an exercise to meet this problem: People in the group make up unreasonable rules. Then, other members of the group break various rules. The person who made up each rule tells the others to stop breaking her or his rule and why. The group flatly refuses to stop what they are doing and then explains why also. (This exercise is good for anyone who went to school in this country.)

A: No touching.

(People in the group start touching each other.)

A: People will think you are gay.

GROUP: Touching doesn't necessarily mean that I'm gay; and, anyhow, people can be gay if they want to be.

A: Keep your distance.

GROUP: I would rather be close.

A: People will think you are weak.

GROUP: They're wrong.

A: Keep to yourself.

GROUP: No, I don't want to do it alone. I *want* to be close.

A: It doesn't look good to me.

GROUP: That's *your* problem!

B: New rule: address everyone as sir or madam.

(Everyone in group starts calling each other by first names.)

B: Respect status. Respect authority.

GROUP: I reserve my respect for things I think are worthwhile.

B: Don't assume familiarity.

GROUP: I want to be close and have human relationships.

B: I'm running the show.

GROUP: I'm not one-down to you.

B: People should keep their distance.

GROUP: I will choose my closeness.

B: That's the way it is around here.

GROUP: Then it's time for a change.

C: A new rule: both feet must be kept on the floor.

GROUP: Breaks rule, etc.

D: A new rule: keep quiet!

GROUP: Breaks rule, etc.

STRUGGLE

In radical psychiatry it is felt that people should not "pig" themselves, and that guilt does not benefit anybody. This is not to say that bad experiences should be ignored or discounted. There are many things that Vietnam veterans may have done in their war experiences about which they will *never* feel good, even after they stop "pigging" themselves about them. Often they have done irreversible damage as part of the United States military. However, veterans can learn from their experiences and put their knowledge to use. They can talk about what they have been doing and become part of a movement which helps make it so that no other people will be cast into the roles they were in and forced to do the things they have done. They can feel better as part of a force which aims at preventing invasions like the one of Vietnam. Permission to be involved in a social struggle can be important in helping a veteran to feel like he is recovering some of his humanity which was ripped off in Vietnam.

Much of the potency developed by group members in radical psychiatry is directed against the oppression which immediately threatens a person. People leave groups feeling capable of handling most problems. In contrast with this defensive potency, social involvement is a chance to take the offensive and strike out against oppression. It serves the function of helping people feel better about bad things they have done by trying to end the roles which oppressed them. Involvement in a social struggle is a good way to feel a part of the human race. Alienation from the human race is not uncommon, especially among Vietnam veterans. To rejoin the human race is to work with other people for a world which is better for everyone, where people can think and love to their full potential.

15. RADICAL PSYCHIATRY AND MOVEMENT GROUPS PLUS A POSTSCRIPT by Claude Steiner

Radical psychiatry's main goal is to help human beings overcome alienation. Because alienation requires contact with other human beings in groups, it is important that radical psychiatry provide guidelines for the healthy functioning and survival of groups. When people who are interested in radical changes organize groups, they quite naturally wish to organize them along lines which differ from the authoritarian and alienating basis on which oppressive, establishment groups are usually organized. As a consequence, the structure of such groups is usually uncertain and indeterminate, and the cohesiveness of such groups against external attack is weak. There are two types of attacks upon movement groups which have become classic examples: one of them is the leveling of hierarchies; the other is the game "Lefter Than Thou."

LEFTER THAN THOU[1]

It is a phenomenon completely familiar to everyone who has worked in a radical organization that in the

[1] This game was first detected by Hogie Wyckoff, who also provided its name.

course of events it often happens that one or more people will attack the leadership by professing to be more revolutionary or more radical than that leadership. Since it is always possible that this is the actual state of affairs—namely, that the leadership of the group has become counter-revolutionary—many an organization has been totally torn apart by this kind of argument; in many cases, organizations that were doing true and valuable revolutionary work.

How is one to distinguish between a situation in which a splinter group is for some reason or another attacking the leadership illegitimately, and one where such a group is, in fact, justified in its attacks?

I would like to cast the illegitimate attack of the leadership of a group by a splinter group in the mold of a Bernian game. The game is called "Lefter Than Thou." The thesis of the game is that a group of people doing revolutionary work which has a certain amount of momentum always includes a subgroup of people with revolutionary aspirations who are nevertheless incapable of mustering either the energy or the courage to actually engage in such activities.

"Lefter Than Thou" players are persons who are dominated by an extremely intolerant and demanding conscience (or Parent) on the one hand and are not able to mobilize their scared Child to do any work on the other. Criticism of the activities of the group and the decisions of the leaders becomes a substitute for revolutionary work. This criticism occurs, usually, at meetings where work would ordinarily be discussed, and it always replaces effective action. "Lefter Than Thou" players are either effective in dismembering the organization, in which case they wind up without a context in which to work; or else they are expelled from the organization by the effective leadership of it, and find themselves again in a situation in which no work can be done.

In both cases, they have a clear-cut justification for their lack of activity, and this is the payoff of the game.

It is a hallmark of "Lefter Than Thou" players that they are angry, often "Angrier Than Thou"; it is quite possible, however, to distinguish the anger of a "Lefter Than Thou" player from the anger of a person who is effectively reacting to his oppression.

"Lefter Than Thou" players are most always children of the middle class. On this basis it is easy to see why a group of black militants can hardly be accused of playing "Lefter Than Thou" while a group of white college students who accuse these black militants of not being radical enough is suspect.

Whether a person plays "Lefter Than Thou" or not can be determined by making a simple assessment of how much revolutionary action they take other than at meetings over, say, a period of a week. It will be seen that, if observed closely, the activity of a "Lefter Than Thou" player occurs mostly in the form of an itellectual "head trip" at meetings and hardly ever in the real world. "Lefter Than Thou" players will excel in destructive arguments, or sporadic destructive action when sparked or impelled by others. It will also be seen that they lack the capacity to gather momentum in creative or building work and that they lack the capacity to work alone due to the extreme intransigence of the Pig Parent in their head which will defeat, before it is born, every positive, life-giving effort.

It appears, therefore, as if that extraordinarily divisive game "Lefter Than Thou" is played by persons whose oppression has been largely oppression of the mind. This form of intellectual oppression, a Calvinist "morality of the intellect," is usually accomplished in a liberal context in the absence of societal or familial application of force—a context in which action or force is actually disavowed, so that the chains that bind the person are strictly psychological or within the head, yet most paralyzing indeed. When anger is felt it is not expressed physically but in the form of destructive talk.

Movement groups are especially vulnerable to destructive talk as their leaders are often in awe of and mystified by intellectual accomplishment. It must be remembered that a game has to be played by the Victim as well as the Persecutor; the Victim in this case being the leaders of the group under attack who, ordinarily, are more than willing to submit to the persecution of the "Lefter Than Thou" player. This willingness to respond to "head trips" and intellectual arguments is a characteristic of certain cultural subgroups, so that while a "Lefter Than Thou" player would be scoffed at and ignored in a very clearly action-oriented movement group, "Lefter Than Thou" players have a capacity to affect the decisiveness of the guilt-ridden intelligentsia.

This game is a liberal, intellectualized form of the aggressiveness that has been observed among the oppressed poor and the blacks. It is a well documented fact that crimes against persons occur mostly between members of oppressed subcultures. Frantz Fanon in *The Wretched of the Earth* illustrates how the savage, homicidal, and capricious criminality that has been observed among Algerians dissolved when the war of liberation became established. The supposed fact that Algerians are born criminals, such being taught even to Algerians by the faculty of Algiers, was not only *not* a fact but a mystification of their oppression. The actual fact of the matter is that the oppressed, when they have no access to their oppressors, either because their oppression is mystified or because their oppressors are not within reach, are likely to wind up at each other's throats. "Lefter Than Thou" is a case of the frustrated and mystified oppressed seizing the throats of their own brothers and sisters because of an incapacity to engage in positive creative revolutionary action.

The measure of a revolutionary's worth is the work

that she or he does. When a person questions the effectiveness of the leadership of a group or the work of a group, the first question to that person should be, "What work are *you* doing?" It will be found that in most cases the critic is a person who is doing very little or no work. If that person is, in fact, contributing a great deal of work outside of the discussions at meetings, then the challenge of the validity of the leadership's goals and methods is again open to consideration. Thus, the demystification of a critic's actual work output is a very important tool in the maintenance of a cohesive movement group.

Another usual attack upon movement groups which is also quite effective is "leveling."

LEVELING, HIERARCHIES AND LEADERSHIP

The greatest single evil in mankind is the oppression of human being by human being. Oppression ordinarily expresses itself in the form of hierarchical situations in which one person makes decisions for others. It has been the wish of many to eradicate this greatest of all evils from their lives. In order to do so, some people have completely leveled hierarchical situations and have attempted to function socially in the total absence of leadership, with the hope of building a society without hierarchies in which the greatest evil—oppression—cannot find a breeding ground.

With the specter of the worst pig, authorization hierarchy, haunting them, people have attempted to work in organizations which have been leveled of all hierarchies. In my opinion, such organizations, when they involve more than about eight persons, have an extremely low chance of survival. When "levelers" enter an organization and impose willy-nilly a no-hierarchies principle, they usually bring about the ultimate destruction of the group.

I will attempt here to demonstrate the fallacy of leveling of hierarchies, as well as to present an alternative to leveling which, I believe, is capable of making rational use of the valuable qualities of leadership in people, while at the same time preventing that extension of leadership into oppression which is such a scourge upon humankind.

First, let me define some terms:

I will call "oppression" the domination force or threats of force of one person by another.

I will call "leveling" a situation in which, at least publicly, no leader is recognized and no hierarchy is allowed in a group, even though leadership and hierarchy may in fact exist.

I will call a "hierarchy" a situation in which one human being makes decisions for other human beings.

I will call a "leader" a person in a group who is seen as possessing a skill or quality which causes others to wish to learn or profit from that quality.

Hierarchies come in a great variety of forms—from the murderous hierarchies in a capricious war to the mother-child hierarchy, including the hierarchies between teacher and student, man and woman, black and white, master and slave, factory owner and exploited worker, foreman and journeyman, craftsman and apprentice. Some of these hierarchies are alienating and dehumanizing. Others are not. To relate to all hierarchies as if they were all dehumanizing and evil is a great error, bordering on mindlessness. Hierarchies should be analyzed in terms of whether they affect human beings well or badly.

There are at least three human hierarchies which are of obvious value, and whose leveling would clearly not profit humankind.

The first and most basic hierarchy is the hierarchy between mother and child. Here, one person makes decisions for another person; and yet it is difficult to see how leveling this hierarchy would be of any advantage. When this mother-child or parent-child hierarchy is extended beyond its fruitful and natural reach—namely, when it is imposed by force or threats of force and beyond the period in which the child needs parental protection and when it is extended to large aggregations of people—then this parent-child hierarchy becomes the model for the military, the great corporations, and so on.

Another such is the hierarchy between a human being who is in great physical pain or need (the sick, the hungry, the wounded, the deranged) and another human being who has the means to fulfill that need. When a person is in dire physical need he may wish that another human being make decisions for him. Again, this natural hierarchy, which is conducive to well-being, can be extended into one that is damaging, as has been the case with the hierarchy that has been created by the medical profession and the attending psychiatric and other mental health professions. Again, the continuation of the need beyond necessity, the continuation of ministration beyond necessity, and the encouragement of the preservation of the hierarchy even in the absence of physical need have resulted in a hierarchical medical establishment which at this point may be doing more against human health than for it. This may sound startling; but if one separates medical knowledge, which is vast and potentially helpful, from medical activity, which is self-serving and oppressive, one can see that the medical establishment is not only not fully serving humanity but holding back potential help from it.

A third hierarchy is based on differences of skill between human beings, in which one person who can be considered a craftsman is sought out by another person who wishes to learn her craft. This hierarchy in which one person places himself below the other in knowledge is desirable to both. The apprentice, by recognizing his need to learn and by riveting his attention to his master, is likely to acquire a skill more quickly and more thoroughly than a student who questions her master's knowledge. On the other hand, a teacher who is given attention and recognition by an apprentice finds in his teaching the greatest reward for his life effort. Both the craftsman and the apprentice profit from this process; and it is hard to see how either of them, especially the student, is damaged by it. Again, this natural hierarchical situation can be extended beyond its necessity, so that certain persons are forever kept in an inferior position to others with respect to their skill. This, of course, is the basis for most universities and professional schools and is again an example of where a natural hierarchy can be extended into an oppressive and evil one.

It is characteristic of humanizing hierarchies that they are, first, voluntary; and, second, bent upon their own destruction of self-dissolving.

All three of the above-mentioned beneficial hierarchies can be extended into oppressive ones. The tendency toward dehumanizing hierarchies that may exist in human beings can be overcome by human beings who decide that they wish to do so. That very same tendency can also be empowered by the human intelligence, as has been done, to the point of building monstrous hierarchies which may now consume us. As human beings we have the choice between mindlessly extending natural hierarchies to the point that they will devour us, or equally as mindlessly leveling and abolishing them; or, on the other hand, using our intelligence, wherever it suits us, to create groups with humanizing beneficial hierarchies when needed.

I wish to postulate an intelligent principle of authority which discriminates between hierarchy and oppression and which, I hope, will be useful to people working in Movement organizations.

The first principle of human hierarchies is that they be voluntary and that they be self-dissolving; that is, that the eventual historical outcome of the group's work be to make the hierarchy unnecessary.

The second principle of human hierarchies is that leaders shall be responsive and responsible.

In order for a hierarchy to be voluntary it cannot involve oppression or coercion by force or threats of force. As a consequence, no one shall use force or threats of force in any situation relating to human beings within a movement or an organization of which they are members. Intimidation of group members by psychological means ("pigging") must be avoided by developing an atmosphere of mutual protection between group members.

Responsive leaders are leaders who are available for criticism by group members. Thus, leadership can be extended only as far as it remains possible for all group members to make extended face-to-face contact with the leaders.

Finally, a responsible leader is one who feels the impact of his or her actions and takes responsibility for them. This is a human quality which can only be assessed by observation. Responsibility is judged from the leader's previous actions and can only be ascertained over a period of time during which his or her work is open to scrutiny and during which the important quality of responsibility is observed.

The same kind of guilt that operates in the leadership when faced with "Lefter Than Thou" players comes into effect when confronted with a leveler.

The self-doubt of a leader is the greatest aid to the leveler. Oppressors don't respond to such attacks at all; but good leaders are prone, because of their basic wish to be responsive and responsible, to allow the attacks of a few to vitiate their useful work for the many. Thus, when faced with such attacks, leaders should responsibly investigate their work and responsively obtain feedback from all the group's members before abdicating their leadership. Only if this analysis reinforces the levelers' arguments should a leader allow that most precarious process, leveling, to occur in the group.

A POSTSCRIPT (1974)

As the editor of this anthology and the originator (some say "father") of Radical Psychiatry, I feel compelled to make a few final statements which come to mind upon rereading this final chapter.

The years between 1969 and 1973, when I finally extricated myself from the position of leadership at the Berkeley Radical Psychiatry Center, have been the most exhilarating, traumatic, dramatic, informative, discouraging, and ecstatically happy, as well as unhappy, years of my life. Looking back, I feel that I've learned a great deal about the processes that govern the formation and development of movement groups and the pressures impinging upon their leaders.

The most important lesson I've learned is in relation to power—and the almost inevitable quandary in which a leader finds herself or himself after whatever movement she or he has originated gains some momentum. My position at the Radical Psychiatry Center after it became a strong organization was very much like the position of the father of an adolescent. I was deeply loved for my good deeds and violently hated for my misdeeds, at times by the same people. And it appeared that as long as I held any power within the radical psychiatry community, I would not be able to live in peace within it. I could not be seen as an equal by others because I had, in fact, a great deal of power. I was not able to give up this power because people relied on it, even as they resented my having it; and also because I did not really know how to give it up effectively. For instance, I was a skilled and experienced therapist, but people resented the manner in which I taught my skills. The only thing I knew to do was to stop teaching, which was in turn resented. Or, I personally held title to the building which housed the Center. This was resented, but the organization was not financially capable of taking it off my hands, nor were they willing to move to a different location. Because I was committed to the eventual equalization of power between all members of the community, I did not hold on to my position as I probably could have, had I wanted to. On the other hand, the ever-increasing stream of criticism and dissatisfaction expressed to me by members of the community as I relinquished my powerful position within it (criticism which they had harbored secretly and had never expressed) became persecutory toward me in magnitude and succeeded in causing me to want to abandon my place within the community altogether.

This process was extremely painful. In retrospect, I wish I had left earlier and thus subjected myself to less pain. The outcome of an earlier departure would not have, in my mind, been to the Center's detriment. I believe now that persons who start organizations should plan how they will take their leave from them before they are forced out; or, heaven forbid, before they find themselves misusing their power in order to hold on to their position. I believe that their main contribution is the forbearance of the wounds sustained in their struggle with their brothers and sisters within the movement. The Radical Psychiatry Center and the Radical Psychiatry Movement, together with the Radical Therapy Movement, have made a profound impression on the psychiatric and mental health professions by now. On the whole, I am satisfied with my contribution to it.

To the people that I struggled with, the people that I loved and benefited, the people that I hated and hurt, I say: "When everything is said and done, the question that remains is simply: 'Have we succeeded in diminishing the oppressive misuse of power by the psychiatric establishment?'; and if the answer is yes, let's congratulate ourselves, one and all."

I believe the answer is: Yes! and I praise us for our accomplishments. Our work continues as the oppression, mystification, and alienation of the people has only begun to be lifted.

Venceremos!

—Claude Steiner
April, 1974

Appendix

APPENDIX A Résumé of the Criticisms of Radical Psychiatry Made by the New Radical Psychiatry Group (November, 1971)

CHANGE

Eight or nine months ago some important changes took place in radical psychiatry: training groups became collectives; we went from being radical psychiatrists to community organizers; and affinity became an important concept. The separation between work and our personal lives became blurred. Using rules learned in intimate relationships we began working on building a utopian community. Our personal lives became a revolutionary testing ground, especially in the sexual areas. The decisions to change were made by a small in-group, yet everyone was *expected* to conform.

POWER

How did it come about that *one group* has the *power*? This evolved as a natural process first by doing together, then sleeping, and ultimately living with one another. People began to look alike and move together. They had the power of getting strokes from each other; they could all vote as a block; they had the power of influence and quick communication. They had the power of allegiance based on sexual relationships. This in-group had created standards for living for the out-group just as in outside society where one group dictates and the rest of the people are isolated individuals. The in-group labels people, calls them "passive power players," "lefter than thou players," "liberal," and makes them feel not O.K. It has become hard to get into training groups and difficult to start a group. Diversity and creativity are stifled. It has become difficult to have criticism heard.

The initial structure of radical psychiatry was based on a teaching hierarchy with the teaching collective at the top and action rap at the bottom. This was a natural hierarchy based on knowledge and expertise; but those at the top of the hierarchy now have power which they mystify and which they are not invested in giving up.

We all agree on the Manifesto, Principles, and Working Policy. In the last four or five months there have been no serious innovations. The in-group did a good job of teaching skills and principles, but these skills and principles have been learned now, and they (the in-group) are no longer needed in that position. The skills have been equalized, but the in-group does not want to give up power or move in a dialectic for change.

The in-group has been putting more energy into solving problems for the in-group than in doing problem-solving groups. We want to put therapy ahead of our personal lives. The in-group has created new unstated demands which are no secret—having Child affinity and putting energy into our lives as a higher priority than therapy.

Radical psychiatry has become anti-creative as a result of the power structure. New ideas have been overlooked, or ideas that are suggested have not been heard and have been defended against.

The foundation of radical psychiatry is only dealt with from the top. Behavior control has become instituted. (For example, "Don't point.") People talk alike;

they use the same jargon. There are token changes (like changing the name of stamps to "held resentments"). Paranoid fantasies have become used to control deviant behavior. The statement, "I can't work with you," used to be the beginning of a dialogue and work on mediation. Now it is the end of dialogue. It has become established party line. It has become unsafe to act independently and creatively in radical psychiatry. The fear is to be considered uncooperative or competitive.

PRELIMINARY TRAINING

There is no one clear way to get into preliminary training and training collectives. People attempting to get in are not told what the process is. They feel judged and tested. The burden for initiating all moves is put on people seeking training. They are made to feel powerless and feel pressured to adapt. They feel confused, alone and unsupported, which causes empowering and alienation.

Group members have a difficult time getting into training collectives. They also are oppressed by values in radical psychiatry. They are told that there is only one way to end oppression. Values and ideals are pushed on group members. The assumptions about relationships are anti-monogamous. Values and rules about groups are not explained or encouraged to be questioned. Group members can't play in the same space as group leaders or get training. Leaders do not talk about their own problems or admit they have problems. Group members are told if they don't like it they can leave.

CRITICISM AND COMMUNICATION

People with criticism have been labeled "lefter than thou players," "destructive forces," "uncooperative."

This labeling destroys the dialectic process as it prevents criticism. The biggest offenders are those in power in the in-group. They get strokes from each other, are one-up, and consider themselves better. Issues that they do not like are considered "head trips" and "piggy." There is only one form of criticism allowed: "this feels bad"; and if you don't use it you're told to leave or shut up.

Communication barriers are being used to maintain power. There is horizontal communication, but little vertical access. This maintains the power structure in radical psychiatry. Outsiders can think they've become insiders, but they are still outsiders. For instance, group members asked for a sheet explaining rules about problem-solving groups, but there was very little energy put into this. Group leaders isolate themselves so they don't see the effects of their power.

In action rap there is a lid put on spontaneous feelings. Anger has become "pig," and laughter has become "gallows." In regard to our jargon, we tell people to wait and get used to it. This encourages empowering and adapting. We discount fresh perspectives and reinforce stock responses. The facilitator in action rap will say "I support you," meaning that he gives permission without any real human caring or actual protection. Facilitators maintain power by this double message which is a verbal message not backed by feelings. The facilitator in action rap may be uptight, but says it's O.K. for other people to be open.

SELF-CRITICISM IN RESPONSE TO THE CRITICISM OF THE NEW RADICAL PSYCHIATRY GROUP

Distribution of power in the radical psychiatry community is uneven and mystified. Some people have more power than others. Some sub-groups have more power than others. Power resides in strokes, communication, money, affinity, etc. Equalizing power among the various spheres of interest in the radical psychiatry community is essential.

Homogeneity or lack of diversity colludes with empowering. Any homogeneous group becomes empowered by those who see themselves as different from it. We need to share things other than radical psychiatry. There are things outside of radical psychiatry modes that people can give each other.

We need to create a sense of *safety, openness,* and *desire for change* so that criticism is freely given, as well as desired, heard, and implemented.

We have to figure out how to work with antagonistic criticism, and we have to learn to distinguish antagonistic criticism from cooperative criticism.

We have to work on being open to and encouraging feedback and critical feedback of action rappers, group members, and leaders-in-training. We have to make an all-out effort to encourage people to write so as to better disseminate ideas.

Group members need more access to information, specifically radical psychiatry theory.

We have to evaluate the relationship between group members and group leaders and between action rappers and group leaders.

This means, specifically, in terms of strokes, since strokes are power, especially physical strokes, sharing social space, sharing play space.

The stroke economy within the community as well as in relationship to people outside the community needs to be demystified. The relationship between strokes and power needs to be demystified and dealt with.

Often, sexual strokes are empowered. Thus, nonsexual relationships are considered deficient in some way. There's a lack of emphasis and encouragement of brother-to-brother, sister-to-sister, and brother-to-sister relationships.

TRAINING AND PRE-TRAINING

Training and pre-training need heavy criticism, analysis, and change. Pre-training, especially, has developed sloppily and with a great lack of self-criticism and discipline. Much work is needed here.

Should group members be in training at the same time that they are in group?

It's important to watch for the problem or unwillingness to share power in the area of preliminary training. This problem happens a lot, specifically in the relationship between people already in collective and preliminary trainees, and needs to be worked on.

We have to make slots during specific collective periods and problem-solving groups for talking straight. Paranoid fantasies have been used to include much more than paranoid fantasies because of a lack of place for feedback, hunches, intuitions, thoughts, questions, Pig messages, etc. Anger and Pigging has been delivered in the form of stamps at the beginning of meetings. Ritualizing transactions in this way needs to be re-evaluated and re-structured.

Our use of specialized language and specialized ways of relating (stamps, paranoias, no pigging) often isolates us from other people. Our expectations that all our strokes be gotten from people within the community and not from people outside isolates us and is a discount of other people. We don't give enough support to people who work in radical psychiatry who get strokes from people who do not work in radical psychiatry.

CONCLUSIONS

The above self-criticism, a great deal of which comes from and coincides with the New Radical Psychiatry Criticism Seminars, does not necessarily spell out any insoluble differences between them and us.

However, there is one basic political difference between the two groups that we've been able to ascertain from doing an evaluation of their criticism. Primarily the difference manifests itself in terms of how the two groups want to practice radical psychiatry.

The New Radical Psychiatry group seems to want to relate to each other around work only. That is, working in training collective, doing problem-solving groups, doing action rap, and having seminars, but not beyond.

We, on the other hand, want to learn, teach, develop, and *live* Radical Psychiatry. We want to build a supportive, therapeutic, political community in which radical psychiatry theory is practiced. We want to build personal, political, and working affinity, while the New Radical Psychiatry group believes work affinity is all they want. It is because of this very basic difference that we don't want to work with them any longer.

We do not believe that it is necessary to be able to work with everyone to create revolutionary change. It is possible for there to be many parallel struggles in the Radical Therapy Movement.

Index

INDEX